NORTH SHIELDS & TYNEMOUTH PUBS

EILEEN BURNETT

AMBERLEY

Acknowledgements

I would like to thank Julian Harrop of Beamish Open Air Museum of the North, for giving me access and permission to use photographs from their collections. Ron Lawson of Sunderland Antiquarian Society for allowing me to copy photographs from his Vaux and Scottish and Newcastle Breweries collections. Richard Purvis for his help. I am also grateful to the number of landlords, landladies and staff for allowing internal photographs to be taken of their establishments and being so helpful.

Photographs courtesy of Beamish, the living Museum of the North: North Tyneside Planning Department collection; Exchange Hotel, Seven Stars, Union Quay, Robin Hood, Albion Hotel, Bedford Street, both Duke Street, Vaux collection: Central Arms, post card of European and United States Hotel and Albion Hotel.

Photographs courtesy of Ron Lawson; The Rising Sun and Marquis of Granby.

First published 2021

Amberley Publishing
The Hill, Stroud
Gloucestershire, GL5 4EP

www.amberley-books.com

Copyright © Eileen Burnett, 2021
Maps contain Ordnance Survey data.
Crown Copyright and database right, 2020

The right of Eileen Burnett to be identified as the Author of this work has been asserted in accordance with the Copyrights, Designs and Patents Act 1988.

ISBN 978 1 4456 9672 0 (print)
ISBN 978 1 4456 9673 7 (ebook)

British Library Cataloguing in Publication Data.
A catalogue record for this book is available from the British Library.

Origination by Amberley Publishing.
Printed in the UK.

Key

1. Northumberland Arms
2. Golden Fleece/Port Hole
3. The Black Lion
4. The Newcastle Arms
5. The Exchange Hotel
6. Seven Stars
7. Prince of Wales
8. The Newcastle Arms
9. Lord Collingwood Inn
10. The Highlander
11. Staith House
12. Low Lights Tavern
13. How Do You Do
14. Rising Sun
15. Robin Hood
16. Colonel Linskill
17. Marquis of Granby Hotel
18. Albion Hotel
19. Commercial Hotel
20. Garrick's Head
21. Alnwick Castle
22. The Clock Vaults
23. Uncle Tom's Cabin
24. White Hart
25. Central Arms

26. Sir Colin Campbell
27. The Ballarat
28. Mariners Arms
29. Victoria Hotel
30. The Fleet
31. Aquatic Arms
32. Neville Hotel
33. European and United States Hotel
34. Telegraph Hotel
35. Railway Inn
36. Royal Arms
37. North Eastern Hotel
38. Spring Gardens
39. The Top House
40. Old Hundreds Inn
41. Queen's Head
42. Oddfellows
43. Artillery Arms
44. Golden Fleece
45. Victoria Inn
46. Albert Inn
47. The Langley Castle
48. Coburg Inn
49. Tynemouth Lodge
50. Dolphin Inn
51. Star & Garter

52. Cumberland Arms
53. Bath Hotel
54. Percy Arms
55. Salutation Inn
56. Turk's Head
57. Gibraltar Rock
58. Rose of Allendale
59. Grand Hotel
60. Copperfields
61. Park Hotel
62. Spread Eagle
63. The Sportsman
64. Fox Hunter
65. The Wheat Sheaf
66. Cannon Inn
67. Pineapple Inn
68. The Ridges
69. The Redburn
70. Percy Arms
71. Wolsington House
72. Berwick Arms
73. Turk's Head and
74. Phoenix
75. Crane House
76. Ferry Mews

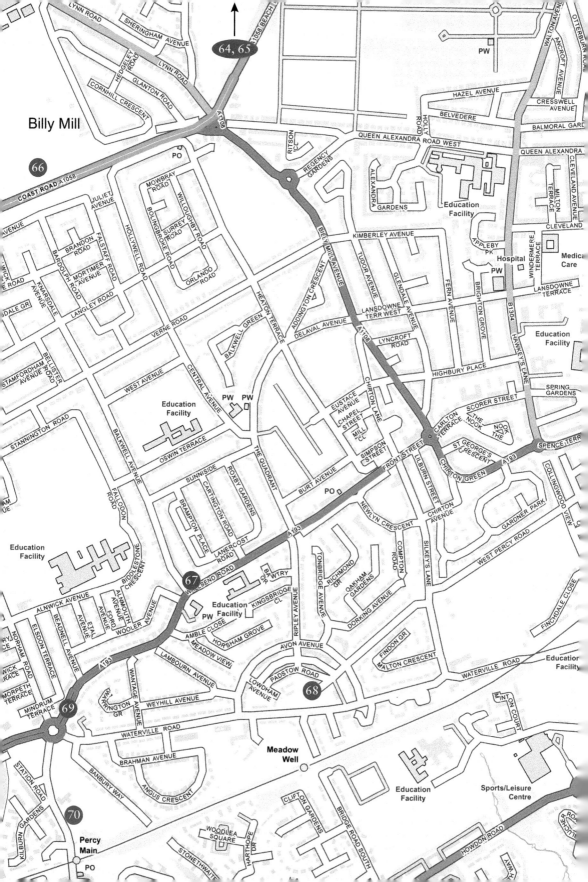

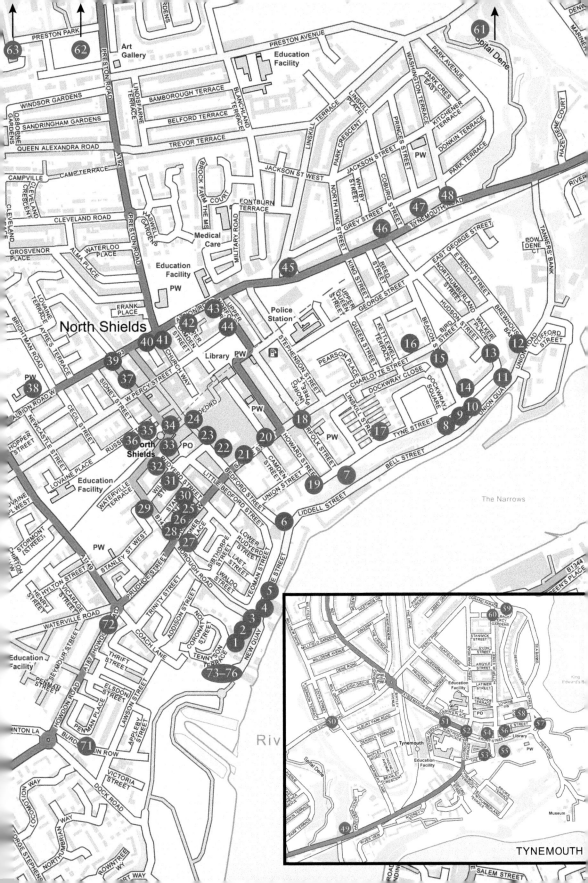

Introduction

This book is about the hotels, inns and taverns in the borough of Tynemouth, which comprises of the town of North Shields and the villages of Chirton (which includes the pit village of Percy Main), Billy Mill, New York and Preston. In the time period I am covering – from 1822 to the present – the separate identities of the communities have eroded by urban sprawl.

In the trade directory of 1872, Chirton was described as being situated as 1.25 miles from North Shields. Percy Main contained two chapels – one Methodist and one Primitive Methodist. St John's Church was described as being 'a handsome building'. The village also boasted a North East Company railway station and an excellent school. Preston, a town and a village only 1 mile from North Shields, had Tynemouth Cemetery open there in 1857. New York, a small hamlet situated around 3 miles north-west from North Shields, contained a Wesleyan chapel.

The book charts a series of walks I took of the area. I made notes of the pub buildings still standing and of ones that are no longer existing. Starting at North Shields ferry landing, I turned east past the Northumberland Arms onto the Fish Quay and up the hill to the main part of the town. I carried along Tynemouth Road onto Tynemouth before turning west to the former villages of Preston, New York, Billy Mill, Chirton and Percy Main before completing the circle back to the ferry landing.

My archival research revealed the oldest public house advertised in the area was the Bee Hive, which was owned by George Kerr in 1754. This was followed by: the Black Lion, registered to John Gilley in 1767; the Half Moon, registered to Mrs Ann Fawdon in 1768; The Sun, registered to Thomas Hampton in 1772; the Fire Engine, known because an auction was held there in 1777; and finally the Black Cock, registered to William Grairs, and the Boat and Coble, registered to Richard Smith, 1787. All of the pubs were registered as North Shields and no street names were given, possibly because the whole road from the Fish Quay to the ferry landing was simply called Low Street.

The area grew rapidly in population and public houses over a hundred years. By 1894 North Shields, along with Newcastle and South Shields, were called the three most drunken towns in Britain – in proportion to their population.

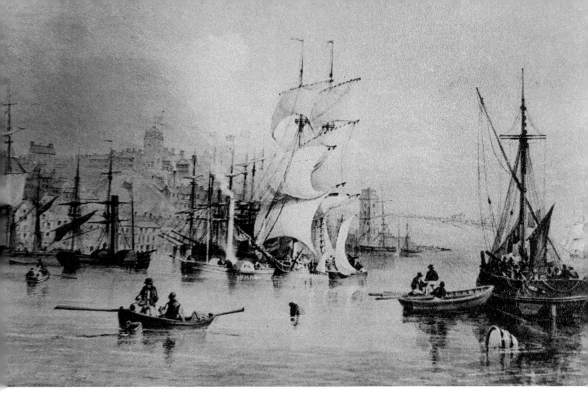

Shields Harbour around 1850.

At Tynemouth Brewster Sessions (annual meetings of the licensing judges who grant, renew and transfer licences to sell intoxicating liquor) held on 24 August 1898, it stated that the borough had no less than one licence house for every 190 inhabitants. Convictions for drunkenness did not flatter North Shields either: 1,581, in comparison with its southern neighbour of only 1,044.

Most of the pubs from that period no longer exist but their presence lives on in the newspapers and reference books of the day.

1. Northumberland Arms

The foundation stone for the building of the new Market Place area was laid on 14 October 1806. Northumberland Arms Inn, a Grade II listed building, was originally one of the homes for the Duke of Northumberland. In 1811 Mrs Carr was the landlady of the inn when Mr Hopper of Tynemouth (bankrupt) made his first dividend payments there on 27 February that year; he was the first of many. Being in a prominent position the inn was well situated to hold auctions. One held on Tuesday 9 June 1812 was for the 'Docks and Ship Building Yards on the Tyne belonging to Francis and Thomas Hurry, deceased'. On Thursday 22 December 1814, the twenty-second birthday of Lord Algernon Percy was celebrated by his friends at the inn. In honour of the recent wedding of Earle Percy to Lady Charlotte Florentia Clive, a party of gentlemen hosted a dinner at the inn on Friday 6 June 1817.

In 1827 Elizabeth Sears advertised the inn for the first time. On Friday 8 November 1828 a large party of tenants of the Duke of Northumberland and gentlemen

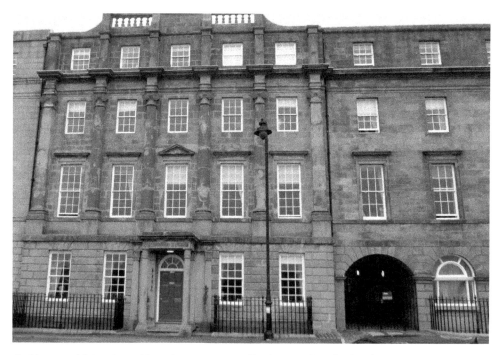

Collingwood Mansions, New Quay – originally the Northumberland Arms Hotel and later known as the 'Jungle'.

residents of the neighbourhood of the boundaries of Tynemouth parish partook of an excellent dinner at the inn. On 30 January 1833 the inn, together with the stables and coaching house, was up to let, having been completely repaired. On 16 May 1833 an advert placed in the *Courant* by Edward Reid and Co. stated, 'The Omnibus leaves Tynemouth for Newcastle ten minutes before every hour, Eight Morning, till Eight Evening.' To avoid disappointment people were asked to secure their seats an hour beforehand at the coach office, which was given as the Northumberland Arms. The return journey, leaving from Sandhill, Newcastle, was every hour from 7 a.m. Being in such a prominent position the inn hosted many meetings of local shipowners, as well as the committees of the Insurance Association over the years. By 1848 Bartleman and Crighton, a North Shields brewery company, had bought the inn and in October they advertised it to let. In 1865 it had become known as a Commercial Hotel with Thomas Smith the licensee. Tragedy struck on 24 February 1870 when a fire took place at the hotel and Mrs Smith the landlady was burnt to death. At the beginning of the last century the hotel had become famous with sailors around the world. Unfortunately, it started to get a bad name and was given the nickname of 'the Jungle', gaining a reputation of a more salubrious nature where clientele could buy anything if they had the money. In January 1989 after consulting the council, UDC and English Heritage, Barratt's the builders submitted plans to turn the hotel into eight luxury flats and build a further twenty on the adjacent car park to match the style of the Grade II listed building. In February 1990 the work on seven luxury flats, which included a two-bedroom penthouse with a rooftop terrace, began.

2. Golden Fleece/Port Hole

Recently known as the Port Hole, this Grade II listed building is at the bottom of Borough Road. The Golden Fleece, originally a much smaller building with another building on either side, gave the address as New Quay and was advertised in 1834 by Robert Hall. By 1838 Samuel Wilson had become the landlord, but sadly in 1839 Samuel died. In August a notice in the *Courant* for all persons who stood indebted to Samuel Wilson were requested to send their accounts with the nature of their security, if any, to Mr Webster, solicitor, Norfolk Street. On Wednesday 14 August an auction was held at the Golden Fleece for all of its possessions, including a quantity of brandy, whisky, rum, wine, bottled and cask porter, ale, along with all the fixtures. The Golden Fleece was up for let in June 1841. Thomas Hogarth was in occupation at the time and Thomas Robson became the landlord in August of that year. In December 1841 Thomas Robson was charged with keeping a disorderly house and was fined 2s 6d (12 $^{1}/_{2}$p) with costs. Samuel Brown took over the inn in 1858 and refurbished the inside, opting for a 'long bar' instead of a traditional layout of smaller taprooms and sitting rooms. Samuel was also instrumental with bringing in glass pots for drinking instead of the pintware that had been traditionally used. In December 1865 an office was opened for the use of the North Sea Pilots within the inn. It proved a popular place, being so close to the ferry landing. On Tuesday 3 May 1887 'Mr Robert Morrison Tate offered for sale several properties, situated in North Shields, in accordance with an order from the High Court of Justice, Chancery division.' This included the Golden Fleece, which was Lot 1. The auction price was £3,000, and the property was knocked down to Mr Bramwell at £4,100. Rebuilt in 1897 the Golden Fleece then occupied the whole of the site of the original three premises. Towards the end of the last century the

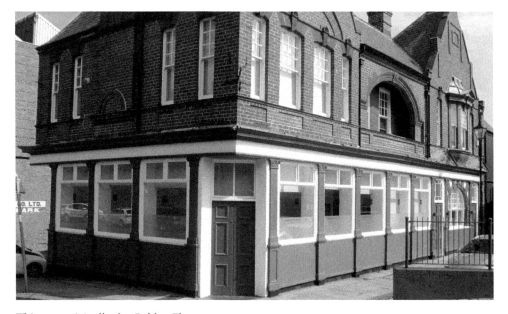

This was originally the Golden Fleece.

Golden Fleece became the Port Hole. Unfortunately, the Port Hole was not attracting enough clientele to sustain business and in February 2015 the firm Blake Hopkinson Architecture turned the 117-year-old building into their new commercial headquarters.

3. The Black Lion

The Black Lion, which stood behind the Port Hole, was advertised by John Dawson in 1822, but is much older. A brig, the *Nightingale* and the ship *Hazard* were sold at auction on Thursday 19 November and Wednesday 24 of November 1767 respectively on the premises when John Gilley was the proprietor. Mary Dawson called it the Black Lion Tavern when she took over in 1844. Then in 1853 Mary called the tavern the Old Black Lion, staying until the beginning of 1860 when P. Stanwix became the licensee. On 16 May 1913 a presentation was made to Mr Joseph Marwick, a member of the Shields passenger ferry, on the occasion of his marriage. Mr Sam Ord made the presentation of a beautiful chiming clock, suitably inscribed – the gift from his many friends. Unfortunately, the four-storey, Georgian-style building with its curved façade was demolished in 1967.

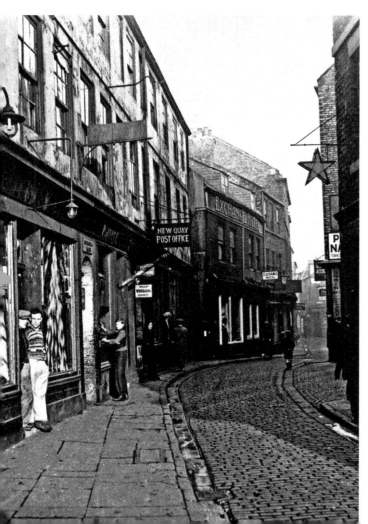

Clive Street *c.* 1931 with the Exchange Vaults just past the post office and the star on the Old Black Lion on the right.

4. The Newcastle Arms

The Newcastle Arms was advertised by Richard R. Storey in 1827, who was also an auctioneer. On Friday 6 February 1829 the Star Cargo Association held their annual general meeting at the inn, the purpose of which was for laying out the terms of the insurance policy, which was to commence on the 20 February. This insurance was against fire, total and partial loss of cargo and freight, or loss by being run aground. Many auctions were held at the Newcastle Arms while Richard was there. By 1834 Richard had left the inn and Margaret Dixon was the licensee. In 1844 George Dobson had added the prefix 'Tavern' to the name, but in 1846 Young Dobson dropped it. Young and George Dobson kept the Newcastle Arms until the beginning of the 1860s when the address was No. 49 Clive Street. In 1865 John Harrison changed the name to the Whitby Arms, and later it possibly became part of the Post Office.

5. The Exchange Hotel

The Exchange Hotel was originally the Waterloo Inn when advertised in 1846 by George Wilson, who gave the address as No. 16 Clive Street. By 1854 Edmond Byron had taken over the inn and in 1859 gave the address as No. 51. On the death of Edmond Byron, his wife Mary Strothard Byron became the licensee, keeping the inn until George Dunlop Adam took over as proprietor in 1874 and renamed it Exchange Inn. In September 1912 an inquest was held into the death of Edward Scully, aged thirty-two, bar manager of the hotel, whose body was found on the railway line. George Geoffrey Alexander, barman at the hotel, told the inquest that they had left the public house at 12.30 a.m. on Sunday then parted at the corner, as Edward Scully was going to take a short cut home. He was found the next morning. In March 1914, while workmen were altering the hotel one of the men, William Thompson, a joiner, was taking up some floorboards and assisting the landlord Fred Connacher to move the counter when he picked up a penny and a halfpenny that had rolled beneath it. Thompson then noticed a loose floorboard; lifting it, he found an old tin box that contained 41 sovereigns belonging to the Victorian era, except for one that dated to the reign of George III (1760–1820). On 13 October 1933, J. W. Cameron & Co. Ltd placed an advert in *Shields Daily News* for the sale by private treaty of the counter, fixtures and fittings of the Exchange Hotel, Clive Street. This signalled the beginning of the closure of the hotel.

6. Seven Stars

Seven Stars, No. 1 Wooden Bridge, stood at the bottom of Lower Bedford Street at its junction with Liddell Street, and according to *Archaelogia Aeliana* Series 3 Volume II it dates back to the 1690s when John Lomax lived there. On Thursday 6 July 1786 the landlord Henry Massey held an auction at the inn for the sale of ships and dwelling houses along the fish market. An advert appears in the *Mercury* in 1817 when Joseph Fallow & Company (wood, brass and musical clock manufacturers) informed the public that they would be taking orders for new clocks and collecting old ones for repair at the inn. Ralph Gillespy was the innkeeper at this time. In 1834 Mary Clarke became the licensee keeping the inn until her son William took it over. In 1846 it is

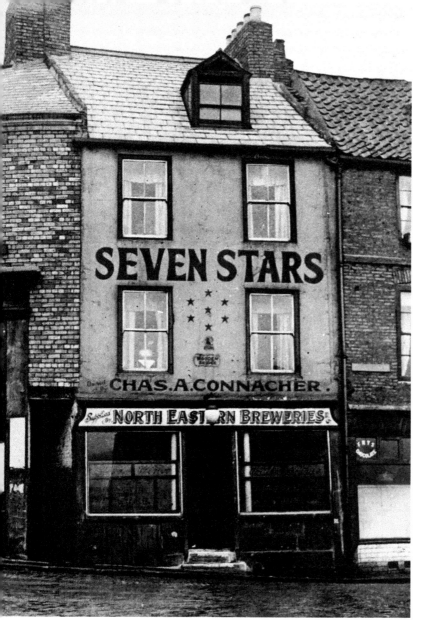

The Seven Stars, No. 1 Wooden Bridge, c. 1920.

registered as belonging to William North Clark and Company, staying in their hands until the end of 1860s when John Johnson, a master mariner, became the licensee. John Johnson did not stay long – possibly his seafaring did not let him devote the time needed to run the inn – as in 1875 John Armstrong became the proprietor. On Tuesday 3 May 1887 Mr Robert Morrison Tate offered several properties for sale situated in North Shields, in accordance with on order from the High Court of Justice, chancery division; this included the Seven Stars at Lot 3. Bidding began at £300. The property was withdrawn at £510 with no reason given. Anthony Nichol Dodds later took over the inn and in 1932 it was owned by North Eastern Breweries Limited and was not advertised after this.

7. Prince of Wales

This was originally the Prince of Wales Feathers when advertised by Walton Emmerson in 1844. Records, however, show the original building dating back to 1674. In June 1842 Walton advertised he was entering into the tavern on Customs House Quay, thanking his friends in the Sunderland Bridge, Clive Street, trusting that they would continue their patronage. On 1 May 1847 the Prince of Wales was up for let – the name

The Prince of Wales Tavern, Liddell Street, and Customs House Quay still has a wooden doll outside.

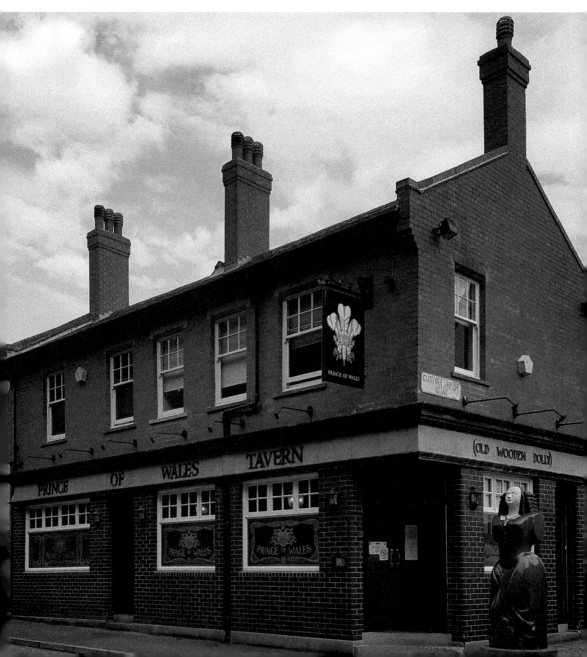

'Feathers' had been dropped. George Slowther became landlord in 1850. On Monday 1 June 1891 the brethren of the Royal Order of Buffaloes held their meeting at the inn at 2 p.m. to take part in the Free Gardeners' Demonstration. A band had been engaged for the use of the brethren. The Buffs, as they are more commonly known, are still in existence today. Owned by consortium Messrs F. R. N. Haswell, J. W. Bramwell and M. Bramwell until bought by W. B. Reid and Co. Ltd on 8 November 1896, who in turn sold it to Scottish Brewers Ltd on 5 May 1959. Due to the decline in the fishing trade many public houses along the Fish Quay suffered and Scottish Breweries closed the pub in 1967. On 30 January 1990 Samuel Smith (of Old Brewery, Tadcaster) bought the former pub, which was being threatened by the road-widening scheme for the new flats being built in the area. Plans had been submitted and rejected. Samuel Smith lodged an appeal against the decision of Tyne and Wear Development Corporation for refusing planning permission to convert the former Wooden Dolly public house, which had been used for a time as a joiner's shop, back into a public house. The appeal was upheld and Samuel Smith was given permission to restore the inn. In February 1992 Samuel Smith opened it as its first northern pub which they had restored to its former glory with very few changes. In 1993 it won the local CAMRA (Campaign for real ale) award. As you walk along from the Ferry you can't miss the green and yellow tiles which adorn the outside with the statue of the Wooden Dolly standing proud next to it. Inside it is split into several rooms and there is a friendly feeling among both staff and clientele. Outside the courtyard has the original cornice stone with the date 1674 and another dated 1927. There is also seating for to sit outside when the weather permits.

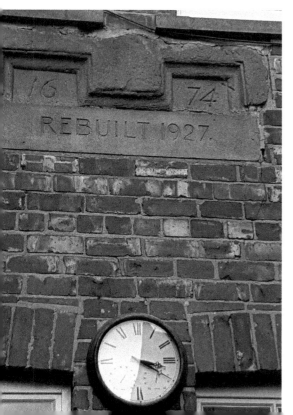

The cornice stone from the original Prince of Wales Feathers, dated 1674, with the one beneath dated 1927 when it was rebuilt.

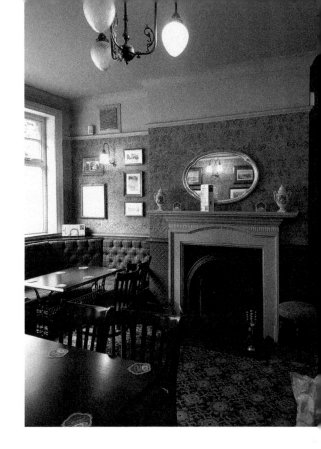

The cosy lounge in the pub.

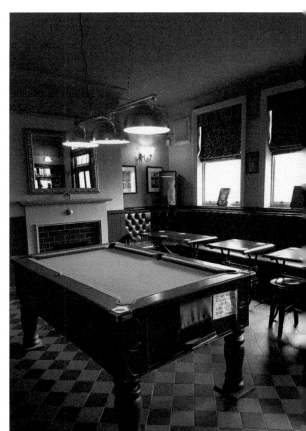

The snooker room.

8. The Newcastle Arms

The Newcastle Arms was advertised by Isabella Thrift in 1827, although on Wednesday 24 February 1819 an auction was held at the house of Mrs Thrift's Newcastle Arms. The inn was in the hands of John R. Smith in 1834, who gave the address as Low Lights. In 1870 James Smith had become the licensee but unfortunately by July 1883 James was to see the inn advertised to let due to his ill health. In September 1905 licence holder Ada Evens Calvert was charged with permitting drunkenness, and her husband with being drunk on the licensed premises on 16 August. On hearing a disturbance, PC Proctor had gone into the premises and found Mr Calvert on the floor very drunk, struggling with William Crane. When questioned Crane told the inspector that he was Mrs Calvert's brother and her husband had been mistreating her and was forcing him (Crane) out of the house. Calvert explained that he had been vexed that his wife had stayed out too long, but had no explanation as to why he was drunk. Mrs Calvert had left her husband in charge while she had gone to the doctor, returning to find him drunk. It was then that he had commenced mistreating her and her brother had become involved. Having admitted the charges Calvert was fined 10s and costs – the maximum penalty. While the justices thought Mrs Calvert should contribute £5 to the poor box and pay costs. This was demolished in 1953 for the building of the Royal National Mission to Deep Sea Fishermen's Hostel.

Newcastle Arms and the Lord Collingwood, Union Quay, *c.* 1930.

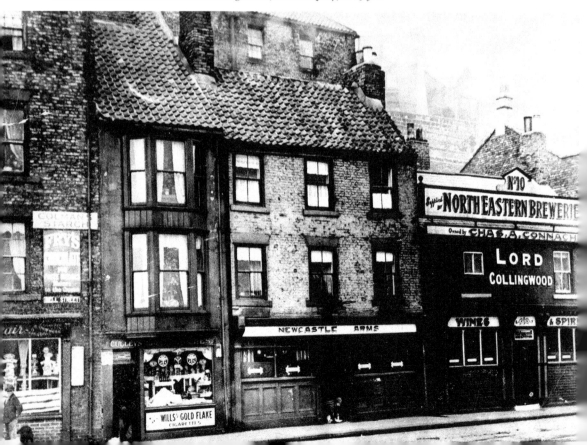

9. Lord Collingwood Inn

William Revely advertised the Lord Collingwood Inn in 1821, giving the address as Lowlights Shore. The inn, which stood at the bottom of Naters Bank, was one of the smaller buildings facing the River Tyne. In October 1871 William Watson was before Tynemouth Magistrates' Court to appeal against a decision to refuse his licence. It was the custom of the Tynemouth borough magistrates to refuse the renewal of a licence if the landlord had two convictions during the previous year, which William Watson had. William Watson had resided at the house and never had a charge against him in all that time – that is until 23 July 1871. He had been away from home when his daughter had admitted some men and children in to shelter from a thunderstorm. The police had found them in the house during prohibited hours. The court thought there was no special reason why they should reverse the decision: the house only had five rooms and they were all small and not suitable for drinking, and there was no yard or conveniences. The neighbourhood was already overstocked with public houses, having one for every three private houses. There were also eight public houses within 100 yards and three within 8 yards. Witnesses were produced by the defence, who argued that during the busiest seasons there would be between 100 and 160 fishing boats lying at the quay and there were not enough pubs to cope with the increase in business. The chairman of the bench

This photograph shows three inns: the Lord Collingwood on the left, the Highlander Hotel next door, and the Rising Sun above, *c.* 1930.

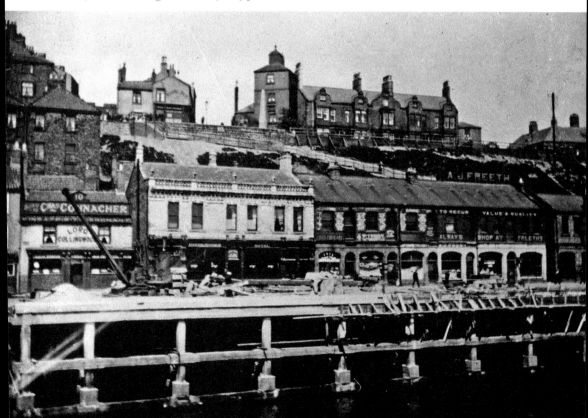

decided to renew the licence. In 1904 the inn was described as having a bar, snug, beer cellar, WC, bedroom, sitting room and kitchen. It became a North Eastern Breweries Limited Inn, eventually becoming a Scottish and Newcastle Breweries inn, more commonly recognised by the sign of the Blue Star. The inn was also demolished 1953 for the building of the hostel for the Royal National Mission to Deep Sea Fishermen.

10. The Highlander

The Highlander Inn facing Union Quay was the largest of the three public houses that stood together facing the river. To the left of the inn you can just see Naters Bank Stairs. When Clark Dixon advertised the inn in 1834 he gave the address as Union Road. Charles Gibson took over the inn in 1846 and in 1848 gave the address as No. 4 Union Road. Charles stayed at the inn for many years and gave the address in 1859 as No. 8 Union Quay. On Thursday 14 February 1884 an auction was held at the inn by W. G. Tate, in which the barque David Malcolm was sold. On 16 October 1890 the Highlander was advertised to let as a free and fully licensed establishment. In March 1920 the Highlander was sold to a Mr Frazer for the sum of £4,000. On Monday 16 October 1933 the body of five-year-old John Fairs had been found by Sidney Styles beneath the Fish Quay. John had been missing from his home, the former licensed Highlander Inn, since 4 October when he had been seen playing on the quay. John Fairs Sr had been the last tenant of the Highlander when it closed and was still living on the premises.

Allard's on the Quay, originally the Highlander Hotel.

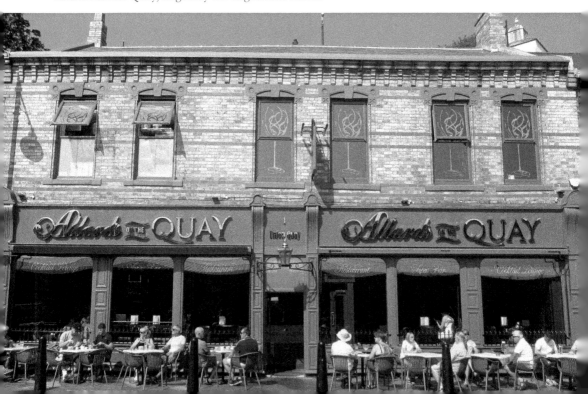

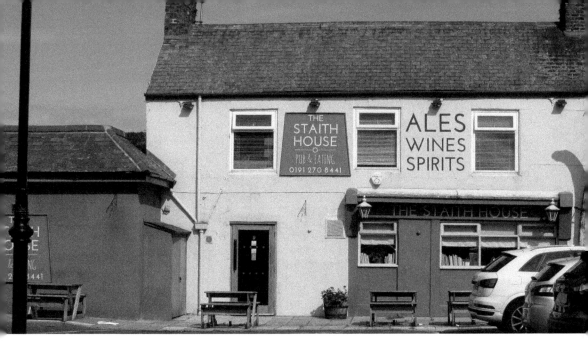

The Staith House, Low Lights, is believed to be over 400 years old.

11. Staith House

Both William Mordue and Andrew Penman advertised Staith House in 1846, but only William Mordue advertised in 1850. Had there been two Staith Houses or just one? It is hard to tell as there were so many inns and taverns in the area at the time. William Mordue stayed at the inn until the late 1850s. In 1858 John Forster, the licensee, renamed the inn the New Dolphin Inn. John had previously been at the Dolphin, Spital Hill, Tynemouth. On Thursday 22 September 1983 Mrs Kathleen Mather, licensee of the Dolphin, was granted an extension to her license from 10 a.m. to 4 p.m. on the Friday and Saturday to coincide with the fish trade exhibition. The police had objected to this as they did not think it warranted an extension since it was such a small enterprise. Two year later and Mrs Elizabeth Mather was granted an extension of her licence – again, from 10 a.m. to 4 p.m. on the Friday and Saturday – to coincide with the fish trade exhibition, which had been organised by Dynoplast. In 1998 the *Star of Peace* fishing boat caught a whale bone in its nets when it was 20 miles off the coast, and it has been beside the pub ever since. Today Staith House is a gastropub and restaurant, serving both lunchtime and evening meals.

12. Low Lights Tavern

The Low Lights Tavern was advertised by John Carr in 1834, when the address was simply Low Lights. It is one of the oldest public houses still trading in North Shields today. On 24 October 1833 Mr J. Taylor, auctioneer, auctioned a fawn-coloured ass, 'suitable for a lady's pad and perfectly gentle in harness', at the tavern. On Wednesday 26 April 1848 at the Commercial Hotel, Howard Street, the tavern along with freehold brewery and plant (containing maltings, stabling, gardens, stack yard dwelling house, offices, cellars and yard) were auctioned by Mr George Marshall. Many inquests were

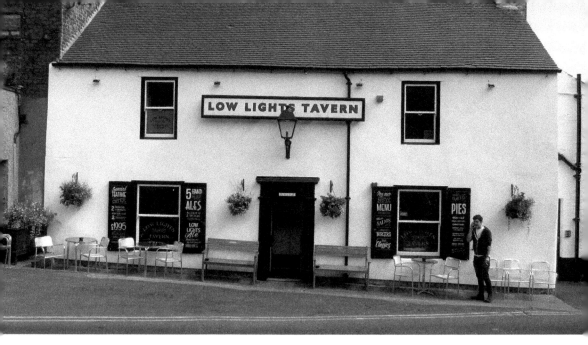

Low Lights Tavern had been trading as an alehouse for more than 400 years.

held at the Low Light Tavern and on Tuesday 30 May 1882 an inquest was held by the deputy coroner, Mr W. Brewis Elsdon, on the body of Hannah Barnsley, aged twenty from Jarrow. The body had been picked up on the Sunday night in the river and had been identified by her father and brother. The verdict was given as suicide by drowning while under a temporary fit of insanity on or around 3 April. On Thursday 21 July 1994 a notice of the application made to Tyne and Wear Development Corporation on behalf of Newcastle Breweries Limited for permission to remove two internal partitions – blocking up one entrance to the bar, along with other alterations that they wished to carry out – were posted in the *Journal* that day. The Low Lights is still open today with a good choice of hand-pulled beers, and Low Lights Ale is made on the Fish Quay. A good selection of food is available, with homemade burgers, salads, the usual classics and their famous pies included on the menu.

13. How Do You Do

Standing near the junction of Hudson Street and Tyne Street, the King's Head would have had a view of the Fish Quay, river and South Shields. When advertised by Thomas Robinson in 1827 he gave the address as Walker Place. Ann Owen in 1844 gave the address as Adamson Place, and Hudson Street in 1846. Arthur Stoker took over the inn in 1850, staying until 1866 when Thomas Stoker became the licensee. On Friday 11 January 1867 the Order of Free Gardeners held an open house at Brother Thomas Stoker's King's Head where candidates were initiated into the mysteries of the order, after which the host provided a substantial supper. By 1900 Westoe Breweries, South Shields, were the hotel owners. On Wednesday 24 February 1943 manager Matthew Baker was summoned by Tynemouth Court for unlawfully harbouring bottles of rum that had not been customed with the intent to defraud the government of duty

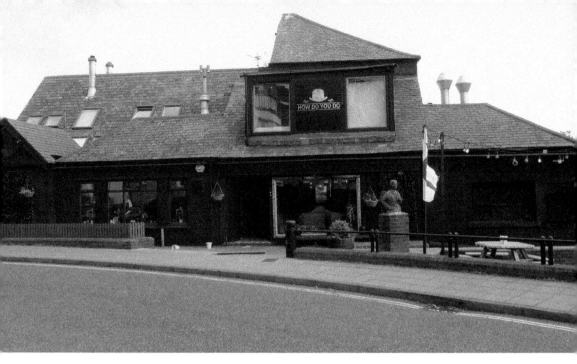

The How Do You Do, Hudson Street, with the bust of a fisherwoman outside.

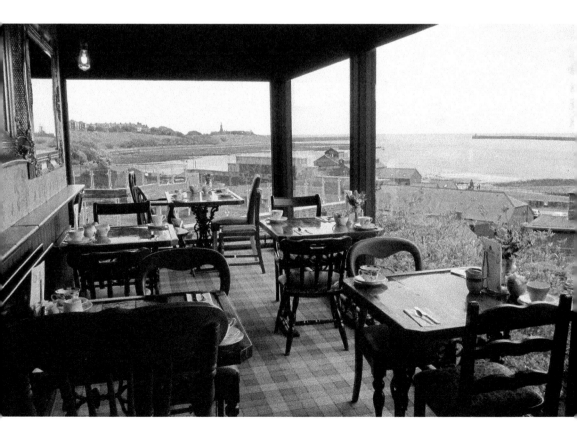

A beautiful view from the dining room window.

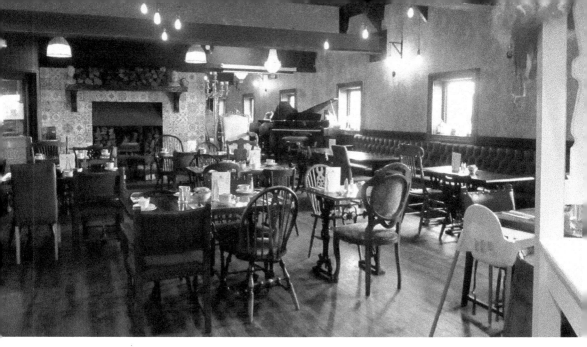

This dining area has a mixture of tables and chairs; the dais has a grand piano for live entertainment.

on 20 November 1942. Another summons alleged he was also dealing with 10 lb of tobacco and 18 pints of rum between 1 December 1941 and 1 December 1942 with the intent of defrauding the government of duty. Matthew Baker pleaded guilty and was fined £10 for each case. Having had many alterations over the years and two name changes (first changing to the Wooden Dolly during the 1990s in a bid to revive its popularity), it also put on live music and became a popular place for musicians. In 2005 the magnificent view from the dining area was almost spoilt by developers wanting to build on the quayside. Today it is known as the How Do You Do and has recently undergone some refurbishment.

14. Rising Sun

Advertised in 1844 by Isabella Archer, the Rising Sun Inn stood on the corner of Beacon Street and Dockray Street, with the High Beacon to the left. In 1846 William Gair had become the licensee, staying until the late 1850s when John Sharp took over the inn in 1859. On Wednesday 2 November 1864 the Ancient Order of Foresters' court falconer let it be known that all the gentlemen who had been proposed and accepted at their last meeting and intended joining before the great soiree were invited to leave their names with John Shay's Rising Sun by the end of the following week, as the court would be assembling only once more before the 21st of the month. John stayed at the inn until his death in 1878, when his wife Isabella became the licensee. On Tuesday 24 January 1893 the inn was put up for auction as the owner Mrs Sharp had recently deceased. It was described as being a 'Freehold Inn and Spirit Bar'. The inn overlooked the estuary, the piers and the sea, and had a frontage of 63 feet. In August that year contractors were asked to tender for alterations that were to be made to the inn. The inn was demolished in the 1960s.

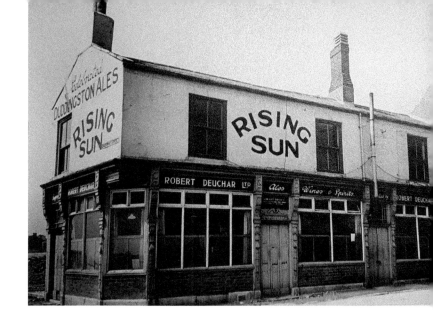

The Rising Sun,
Beacon Street,
May 1960.

15. Robin Hood

Hannah Robson advertised the Robin Hood Inn in 1846 as being in Beacon Street.
By 1850 George Watkins had become the licensee. On Thursday 29 September 1887
an inquest was held at the inn by the coroner J. R. D. Lynn on the body of George
Henry Gillespie, a nineteen-year-old butcher who drowned on Tuesday 27th in the
river by the Fish Quay. After hearing all the evidence, a verdict was given as 'accidently
drowned'. A benefit concert by the Irish Colleens was held at the inn on Thursday
11 March 1927. There was a large attendance who were delighted by the program
submitted by the Dixie Croons concert party. In April 1952 after a fierce thunderstorm
hit the north-east Tynemouth Fire Brigade was called in to pump water out of the inn.
In October 1952 the inn was advertising for a pianist for to play on a Saturday night.
It closed in 1957.

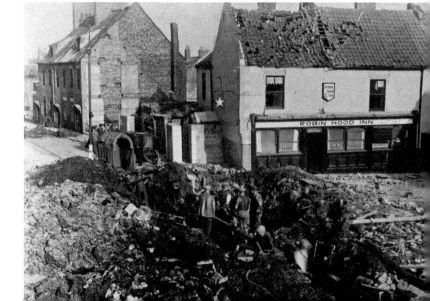

A sad Robin Hood
Inn showing the
damage it sustained
in a bombing raid
during the Second
World War.

16. Colonel Linskill

William Rossiter advertised the Colonel Linskill in 1834, which was at that time a much smaller inn and stood between Harvey's grocery shop and Forster's boot maker and repair shop in a row between King Street and Reed Street according to the 1856 Ordnance Survey map. In January 1887 High Brewery, Duke Street, advertised the inn to let. The original premises were demolished and the present one opened in 1937 with Mr P. C. Smith being the new licensee. In 1939 the mayor of Tynemouth, Councillor Harry Gee, established a fund for the dependants of the crew of the lost trawler *Jeanie Stewart*. By February 1939 the fund had reached nearly £1,700, with Colonel Linskill having contributed £9 18s 3d through their collection boxes. In July 1950 Tynemouth Licensing Magistrates agreed to the transfer of the alehouse, music and singing licence from Stanley Johnson to Horatio John Rhodes, the new licensee. In 1986 the pub changed its name to the Fog on the Tyne, a song made famous by the Northumberland pop group Lindisfarne. On Tuesday 19 February 1991 a quantity of cash was stolen from the inn when a masked raider with a bread knife threatened bar staff wearing dark clothing; he escaped on foot at approximately 6.10 p.m. To rejuvenate the pub its name was changed again, in October 1992, to the Laurel Arms – named after Stan Laurel from the duo Laurel and Hardy. Reverting to its original name, last orders were called in 2013 and all attempts to rent or lease it out had failed. In 2019 a planning application was put forward to North Tyneside Council for approval. If plans are approved the Fat Butcher Steakhouse are going to transform the inn, turning into a shop and offices.

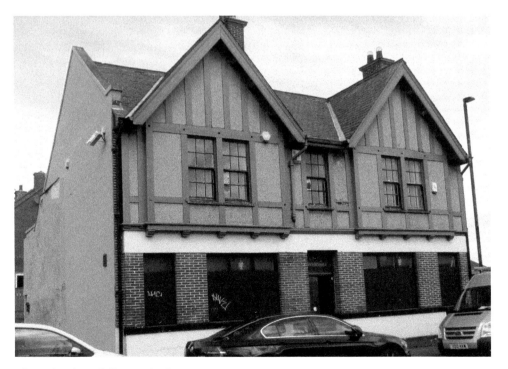

The Colonel Linskill Inn, Charlotte Street.

17. Marquis of Granby Hotel

John Wilson advertised the Marquis of Granby Hotel, on the corner of Church Street and Tyne Street in 1827. In 1841 John Scott became the licensee. On Tuesday 21 December 1841 the brethren of the St George's Lodge of the Free and Accepted Masons held their annual meeting at their lodge room in the hotel for the installation of W. M. Elect (J. W. Mayson Esq.) and the appointment of officers. When John advertised an auction to be held on 16 March 1842 he referred to it as the 'Granby Hotel'. When an advert was placed in the *Courant* for an auction to be held on 17 February 1847, John referred to the Granby as an 'Inn'. During the late 1840s and early 1850s many auctions were held at the hotel – mostly small ships and brigs. On Tuesday 21 April 1940, at Tynemouth Borough Police Court, Charles Richardson, the landlord of the hotel, was fined 40s for failing to obscure lights shining from the three lower panes of the bay window on the premises at 10.40 on 15 April, which meant the light could be seen from the river. On Monday 17 December 1956 Tynemouth Licencing Justices granted the transfer of the licence of the hotel to the Redburn, Percy Main. The transfer had been provisionally agreed in February 1955 and, after inspecting the new public house, was confirmed and took effect at 3 p.m. that day. The application was made by Mr C. P. Rea on behalf of William Younger & Co. Ltd.

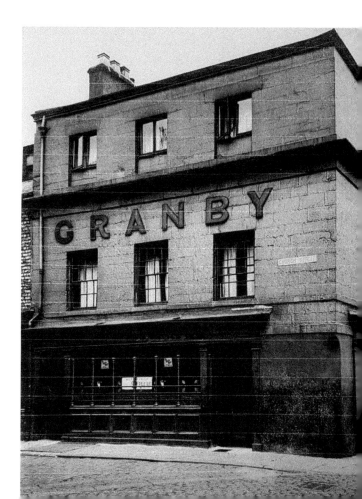

Marquis of Granby Hotel,
Church Street.

18. Albion Hotel

Robert Robson Story first placed an advert for the Albion Hotel in William's 1844 directory thanking friends and the public for past favours, and also to let people know 'a coach for Blyth every morning at half past nine, and every afternoon at half past three, Sunday afternoon excepted. Excellent stabling. A good lock-up Coach House.' We know it is much older than that, however, as an advert in the *Newcastle Courant* placed by Joseph Spark was for an auction at the hotel on Wednesday 29 April 1829, and many more auctions were held there. On 29 September 1831 J. and F. Bell placed an advert announcing to friends and the public that they had taken over the 'hotel' and their 'intentions were to combine comforts of a private dwelling with the independence of an inn', and had carefully selected stock of wines and spirits. When an advert appeared for a 'Dancing Assembly' at the Coach and Horses, Wallsend, on 23 October 1839 tickets were being sold at Mr Storey's Albion Inn. On 18 December 1880 William MacFarlane placed an advert in the *Courant* letting the public know that this first-class family and commercial hotel had now reopened after extensive alterations and an entire refurbishment. On 25 September 1884 Tynemouth Corporation conducted three valuations to settle the value of the part of the hotel they wished to purchase so they could open up the road between Saville Street and Charlotte Street to alleviate the

Looking along Saville Street from Howard Street. The Albion Hotel on Norfolk Street is in the centre of the road.

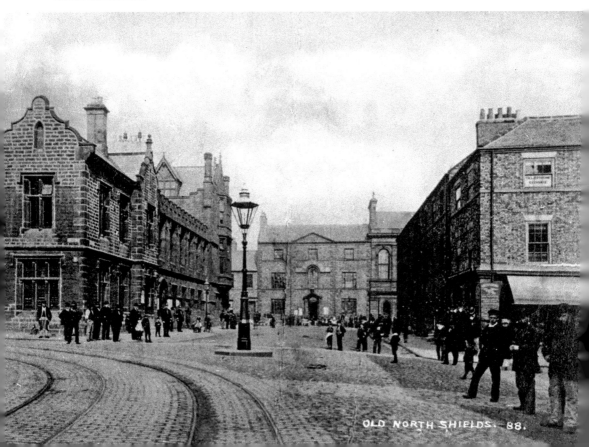

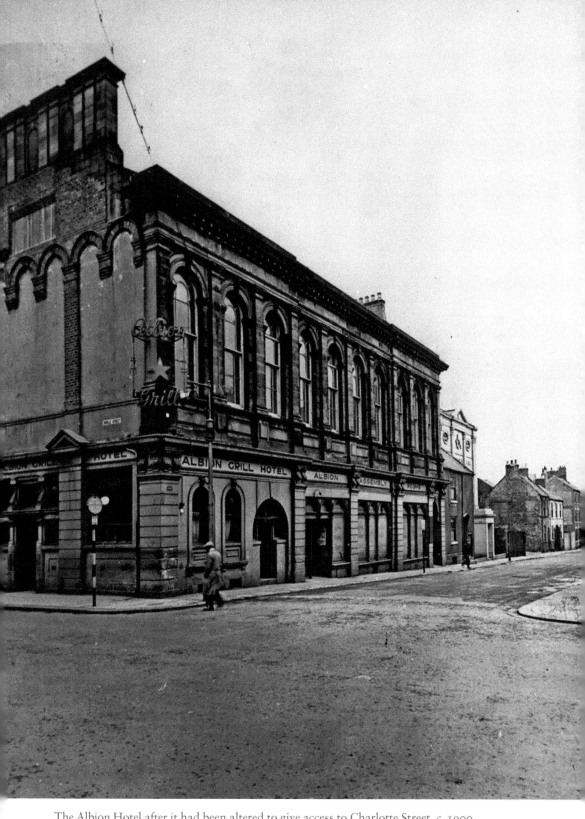

The Albion Hotel after it had been altered to give access to Charlotte Street, *c. 1900*.

congestion on the low road leading to the Fish Quay. Part of the remaining Assembly Rooms was then refurbished to incorporate the hotel and later became known as the Albion Grill. It was closed during the 1970s, and in 1985 was destroyed by fire.

19. Commercial Hotel

This beautiful building was originally built as the Commercial Hotel. William Ward was its proprietor when it was advertised in 1827. The hotel is much older than this, however, as in May 1816 an advert in the *Tyne Mercury* states that William Ward thanked his friends and the general public for favours while he was resident at the Star and Garter and informs them he had moved to the Commercial Hotel, which he

Commercial Hotel, Howard Street.

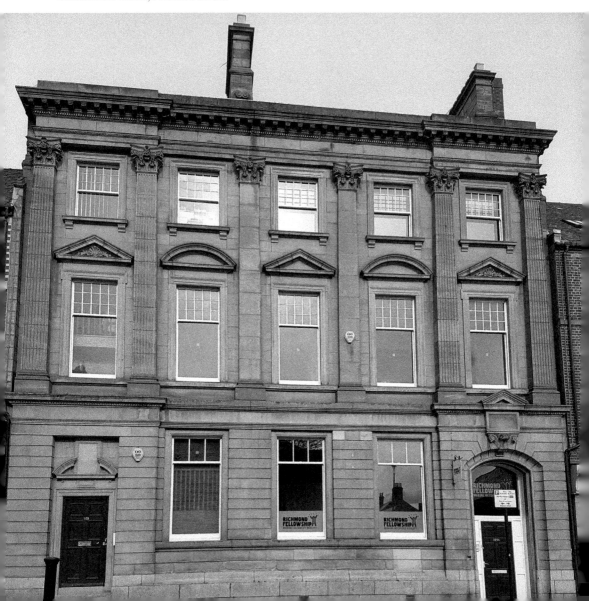

has fitted out in an elegant manner and has a choice assortment of wines and spirits. In December 1819 William Ward advertised 'Mourning Coaches etc., which could be hired on short notice to any port in the kingdom, with good horse, which could be covered in Mourning if required.' On Tuesday 27 October 1829 eight building plots were being auctioned on the west side of Norfolk Street (each being 7 yards from north to south and 16 yards from east to west), with seven sites being auctioned on the east side of Howard Street (each 8 yards from north to south and 21 yards from east to west). This would have been when North Shields was starting to expand into the upper part of the town. On 23 May 1832 Robert Brown informed the 'Nobility, Commercial Gentlemen and Families, that he was removing from the George Tavern, to that Old Established Inn, in Howard Street, The Commercial Hotel'. On Tuesday 15 July 1834 an inquest was held at the hotel before T. W. Keelyside Esquire, coroner, on the body of William Dodds. The deceased fell from the mast of the ship *Palmer*, lying at Peggy's Hole, while rigging the vessel. Verdict was accidental death. William Dodds left a wife and three children. John Dalton had taken over the licence of the hotel by 1846. Thomas Hart was the last licence holder in 1881.

20. Garrick's Head

According to land deeds for July 1807, Thomas Hutchinson was the tenant at the Garrick's Head, Saville Street, while the inn was being held in trust by Joseph Oglvie, chemist and druggist, for Alexander Crighton, gentleman, Howard Street. Margaret

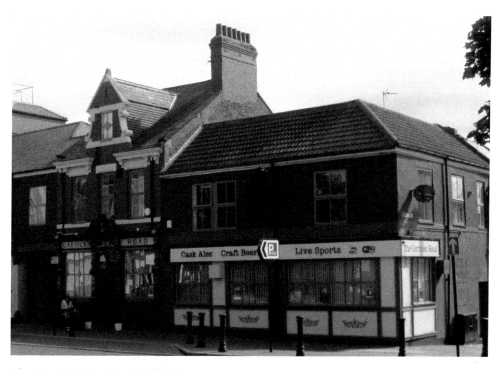

The Garrick's Head Inn, Saville Street.

Lee advertised the Garrick's Head Inn in 1821, which at this time only occupied the site of the three-storey building towards the left of the photograph. William Noble had taken over the inn by 1826 as his wife Ann died there in November of that year. He stayed until 1844 when Henry Kingston became the licensee. Many auctions were held at the inn while Henry Kingston was in occupation. W. H. Reid & Co. Ltd became the owners of the inn, with Harry W. Black becoming the tenant. In December 2001 Garrick's Head was up for sale for £325,000, or to let – terms would be negotiated. There were sales of around £6,000 per week inclusive of VAT. In 2013 Paul Barrass, the tenant of the Garrick's Head, had his licence suspended for ten days following twenty-one incidents of drinking after hours, disorder, drunkenness and anti-social behaviour. On reopening the pub last orders would be called by midnight and everyone was out by 12.30 a.m. on Friday and Saturday nights.

21. Alnwick Castle

James Sproat advertised the Alnwick Castle in 1834, giving the address as No. 22 Church Way. James stayed there until 1857 when Mrs Amelia Lawson became the licensee and the address was now No. 112 Church Way. In September 1883 an extensive amount of wine was stolen from the inn by Robert Henderson (twenty-nine), plasterer; Charles Rowley (thirty-five), cartman; William Patterson (thirty-four), shipwright; and James Creighton (thirty-five), mast maker. They were convicted of stealing more than fifty bottles of wine with a value of over £9, the property of Thomas Dunn the landlord. Each of the prisoners were sentenced to one month in jail. By 1900, Westoe Breweries of South Shields were the owners of the hotel. On Sunday 4 September 1994 fire broke out in the pub just minutes after a fight between customers broke out, with staff having to move everyone out when the fire spread from the yard to the building. Damaged

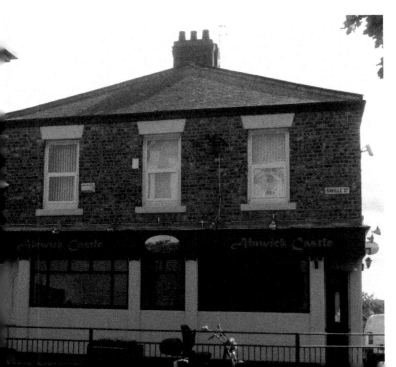

The Alnwick Castle Inn, Saville Street, and Church Way.

was caused to toilets, doors and windows, which also wrecked the beer-cooling system. The Alnwick Castle closed at the end of 2018. It is now Spraatez, an ice cream and frozen yogurt parlour, with the Alnwick Castle coffee shop at the side.

22. The Clock Vaults

The Clock Vaults Inn dominated the corner of Bedford Street and Wellington Street. John William Horsley was the first landlord. On 16 January 1863 Horsley was elected as honorary member of the Licensed Victuallers' Association. On the evening of Thursday 24 November 1864, around fifty of his friends met for a dinner to celebrate the opening of the new long room at the inn. On 8 June 1865 an advert was placed in the *Shields Gazette* and *Daily Telegraph* informing the public that a new large courtroom was open for societies. On Saturday 7 October 1893 the borough of Tynemouth's Leek Club held their seventh annual show in the vaults with fine displays of leeks and a collection of vegetables. On Friday 1 July 1955 Mr J. Limerick, presented a chiming clock to Mr H. Gray, who was retiring after fifty years' service at Smiths Docks, on behalf of the shipwrights. The inn was pulled down in 1968 to make way for the regeneration of the town centre.

23. Uncle Tom's Cabin

Uncle Tom's Cabin was originally called the Railway Tavern and was based at No. 51 Bedford Street when advertised by John Graham in 1846. By 1854 Henry Aynsley had taken over the tavern. In 1859 he is listed as innkeeper and wine and spirit merchant. In 1865 it was known as Uncle Tom's Cabin and the address was then No. 26 Bedford

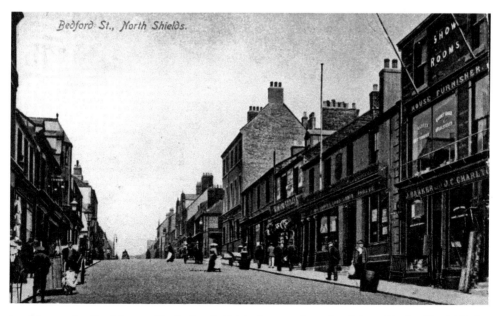

Looking up Bedford Street. Uncle Tom's Cabin is second on the right, with the Clock Vaults (the three-storey building) to the centre of the postcard.

Street. When James Coffee became the manager of the inn he placed an advert in the *Shields Daily News* on Monday 20 June 1898 to inform the public he had done so. In February 1899 a dinner was held for around fifty gentlemen who had been invited by the committee of the North Shields Bicycle Club. The bicycle club had been in existence for twenty years and had made itself known throughout the cycling world. The chairman presented the Percy Cup and a gold medal to Mr Arnold Hunter, who had covered the most miles during the 1898 season. On Wednesday 3 April 1901 a 'Smoking Concert' was held for the members of the North Shields branch of the United Kingdom Society of Amalgamated Smiths and Strickers for the purpose of reorganisation. When the inns music licence was renewed in February 1943 it was agreed that the music and singing was to be by wireless only because of the war. On Tuesday 18 August 1959 a grand reopening of the inn took place after it had been completely modernised and refurbished. In October 1965 Tynemouth Watch Committee approved an application for the installation of a fruit machine, but the public house was not to be around much longer.

24. White Hart

White Hart Hotel, Bedford Street, was advertised in 1844 by William Goldborough. By 1850 G. T Dawson had become its landlord, giving the address as No. 94 Bedford Street. He did not stay long as in 1854 William Atkinson had taken over the premises. In 1873, when Mrs Eliza Cocks took over the inn, it was known as Duffy's Hotel. In

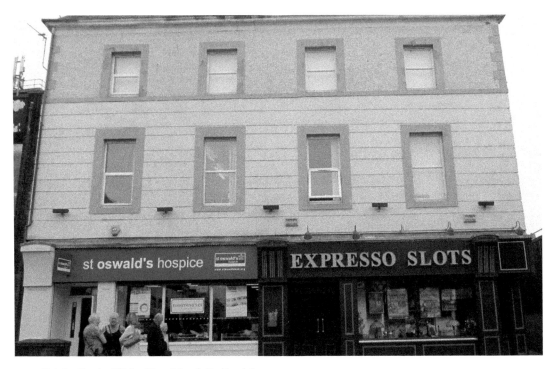

Originally the White Hart Hotel, Bedford Street.

March 1993 the hotel became known as the Cask & Stillage and was listed as one of the top pubs in the area by the *Evening Chronicle*. After a total refurbishment the pub looked great; wood of various hues gave it an 'olde worlde' feel and it had up to date technology. The only thing that had not changed was the warm welcome from the staff behind the bar. It got a reputation for good beer, good food and value for money. Unfortunately, it did not last. On Tuesday 3 July 2001 an enquiry was held in the Cask & Stillage by an inspector appointed by the Secretary of State for the Environment to decide on the appeal against it being converted into an amusement arcade and shop. In February 2002 the shopkeepers in Bedford Street claimed the neglected building was being left to rot because North Tyneside Council had turned down the application by the developers to convert the pub into an amusement arcade and shop.

25. Central Arms

The Central Arms Inn was a small public house sandwiched between the two entrances of what was once the Oddfellows Hall and later the Comedy Theatre in Saville Street West. It was advertised by John Sewell in 1871. On Monday 25 August 1890 a cycling match was arranged. Mr J. E. Willis of the Central Arms took a deposit of £2, binding a 5-mile match for £20 to take place at North Shields Cycling Ground on the Saturday. It was between Thomas Lynn of Percy Main and George Charlton of North Shields. After a very good contest George Charlton almost fell onto the tape. In June 1896 the

Central Arms Inn, No. 6/7 Saville Street West, *c.* 1930.

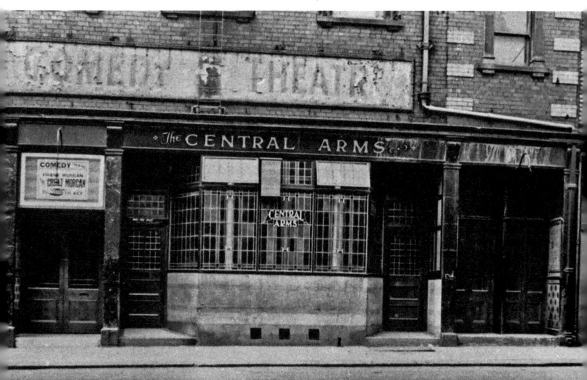

Central Arms was up to let by tender, with the address given as Saville Street West. On Tuesday 18 April 1939 Tynemouth Licencing Justices granted an application made by Durham and Northumberland Licensed Victuallers for alterations to be carried at the Central Arms. This was for the bar to be modernised so drinkers would have more space and it would be easier to supervise. It unfortunately closes not long after.

26. Sir Colin Campbell

This sad-looking building was the Sir Colin Campbell Hotel, first advertised by J. Rutter in 1861. By 1865 Elizabeth Rutter had become the licensee. Robert Y. Robson then took over the hotel. On 1 January 1890 Anthony Nichol Dodds was advertising for the festive season with a large selection of wines and spirits, and special attention given to blended whiskies at 2s 6d (12.5p) and 3s (15p) per bottle. Bottles were guaranteed six to the gallon. In May 1897 A. N. Dodds went before the Music Licenses Committee, applying for singing and music licenses only for the hotel. Clubs met at the hotel most nights in the week and he was applying on their behalf for the facilities for entertainment. On 15 January 1902 the Lily of the Valley Lodge of the National Union of Free Gardeners sat down to their annual supper, after which Brother W. D. Waugh, their secretary, was presented with a marble timepiece suitably

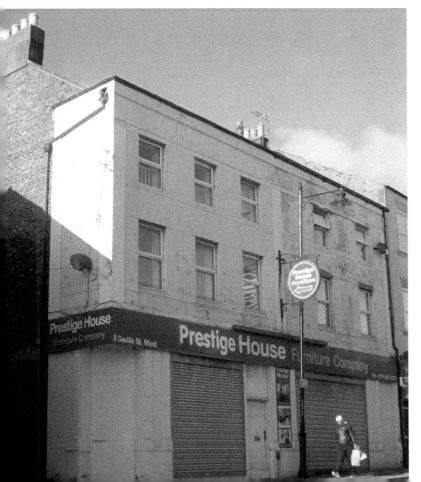

Originally the Sir Colin Campbell, Saville Street West.

inscribed for his twenty-five years in service, along with a pair of bronzes. His wife also received a gold broach presented by Brother Stroud. In July 1922 the first show of the National Irish Terriers Club in the north was held at the hotel, and famous Irish Terriers were present from all parts of the north. The society, which had only been going for a few months, was making great headway. Following complaints by neighbours about the noise from the hotel, a noise-control device was installed at the end of September 1996. Robert Shepherd Bradley, who held the tenancy of the hotel, was declared bankrupt on 6 July 1998.

27. The Ballarat

The Ballarat sits in a prominent place at the top of Borough Road, on its corner with Saville Street West. Thomas John Dodds advertised the Ballarat Hotel in 1872, giving the address as Saville Terrace. In 1875 the address had changed to No. 42 Saville Street West. On Sunday 7 September 1879 Mr Harry Linn had an advert in the *Era* – a London newspaper in which theatrical agents would advertise – and Harry gave his address as the Ballarat, North Shields. At the end of 1936 Newcastle Breweries Limited had the hotel refurbished and redecorated by Chisholm and Company of Upper Reed Street in the town. The design is in buff colour terracotta with the name in red and black letters to give it a more modern look. One of the bars had extensive changes made to transform it into an up to date sitting room with luxurious upholstered sitting accommodation and modern facilities. In 1990 Vic Baddoo became the manager and joint owner of the Ballarat with his mother Betty. In November 2005 the Ballarat closed after the landlord failed to apply for a new license. After being closed for many years the Ballarat was opened once more in October 2012 by Karen Mitchell and is still open today.

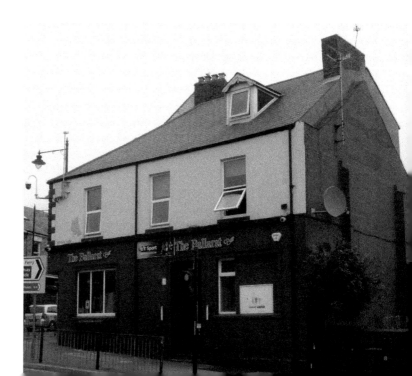

The Ballarat Hotel, Borough Road and Saville Street West.

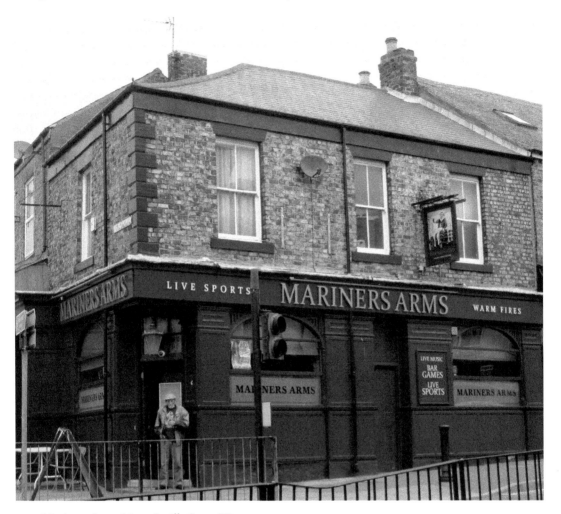

Mariners Arms, No. 1 Saville Street West.

28. Mariners Arms

The Mariners Arms was advertised in 1883 by George Sands, who stayed until around 1888. In subsequent directories despite the address it is mostly advertised as a beer retailer's. In July 1901 a presentation was made to Mr & Mrs John Long of the Black and Gray, South Shields, from his friends at the Mariners Arms, North Shields. On 6 November 1902 John Long died and the notice in the paper stated 'late manager of the Mariners Arms North Shields'. On 21 October 1904 Robert Allison age 35 years, died at the Mariners Arms leaving his wife Elizabeth to carry on the business. It was not until Fras McKay became the licensee in 1938 that the Mariners Arms was again advertised. In May 1951 Judge Richardson granted possession of a dwelling house at the Mariner's Arms to the Newcastle firm John Rowell and Sons Limited and ordered the tenant Mr S. Stephens to vacate the premises within twenty-eight days. The Mariners was originally only an alehouse and unable to sell either wines or spirits until the 1970s when it received a full licence to sell them. After the Mariners Arms was bought from Scottish and Newcastle Brewery by Legendary Yorkshire Heroes managing director Tony Brookes, who was not keen on the name, he decided to have a name change. In June 1990 the Mariner got not only a new landlady but also its new name. Betty Baddoo was not only the owner and new landlady, but also had the pub named after her. Unfortunately, however, the name change was not popular and just over a year later the pub once again became the Mariners Arms.

29. Victoria Hotel

This was advertised by Mary Ann Holt in 1865 as being situated in Borough Road. She then advertised the Victoria in Ward's directory of 1865/6 as being in William Street. On Wednesday 14 January 1885 a supper was held at the hotel in connection with the Ancient and Illustrious Order of the Knights of Malta. On 23 April 1890 Christopher Donaldson died and his wife Mary became the licensee. In June 1891 the hotel was up for let and applications were to be sent to Bell Brothers, Groat Market, Newcastle. At the end of January 1896, the hotel counter with a copper basin and four motion beer engines, along with several beer casks with taps, was for sale at the hotel. In June 1901 the hotel was once again up to let; this time applicants were to apply in person to Bell Brothers. In November 1944 Mr G. McCann gave a £20 contribution to the Tynemouth Infirmary Fund – quite a considerable amount in those days. On Wednesday 23 October 1946 a fire at the hotel on the first floor, which was the living quarters, severely damaged the back room, but was put out within half an hour. The cause of the fire is still unknown. In July 2002 the council's licensing committee granted the pub an entertainment licence to host music and dancing. It is now residential.

Victoria Hotel, Borough Road, and William Street, now residential property.

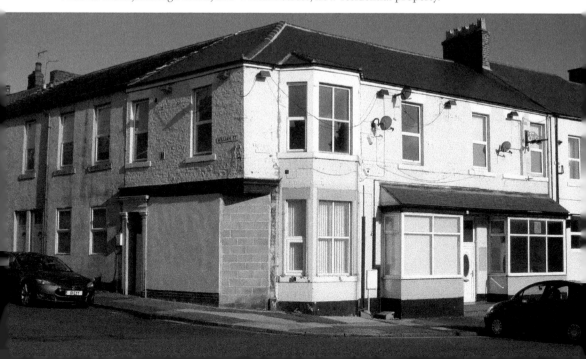

30. The Fleet

The Fleet public house was originally the Stanley Arms when advertised by John Rogers in 1861. In January 1863 John had been elected as an honorary member to the Licensed Victuallers' Association. William Stanley took over the Arms in 1871. The Arms was advertised to let on 27 November 1879 and taken over by Charles Alfred Hughes. In July 1880 John Fitzgerald, wine and spirit merchant, reopened the pub. In March and April 1881 the Arms was host to the Great American Billiard Tournament, which was hosted by William Young; admission to the public was 6d. In March 1883 there was a notice in the *Shields Daily News* that the Stanley Arms was for sale by private treaty, owing to there being a death in the family and the proprietor wishing to retire. William Lilburn became the new licensee. The first meeting of the newly formed Stanley Cycling Club was held on 5 June 1913, for the purpose of electing officials and arranging fixtures for the season. Mr Fred Cook was elected president; William Johnstone, secretary; and George Russell, treasurer. On 28 August 1973 a mysterious blast wrecked the cellar of the pub, injuring the landlord's wife Jean Henderson and barmaid Mrs Esther Durant, who were taken to Tynemouth Infirmary suffering from shock. The blast shook the building; a heavy table was flung 2 feet in the air and a heavy door blown off its hinges. Outside the impact lifted the cover off the cellar hatch in Rudyerd Street. In 2012 the Stanley Arms became known as The Fleet. In March 2017 a proposal was made by JMJ Property Ltd to convert The Fleet into a

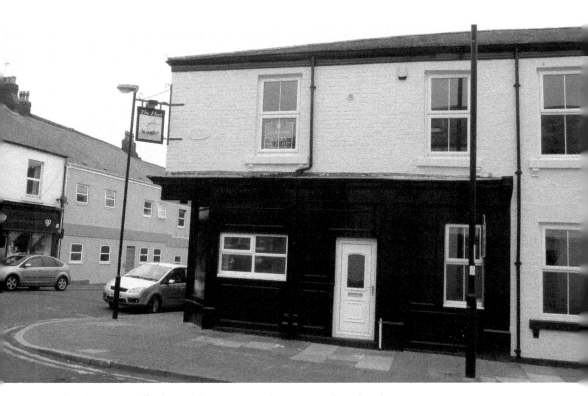

The Fleet, originally the Stanley Arms, Stanley Street and Rudyerd Street.

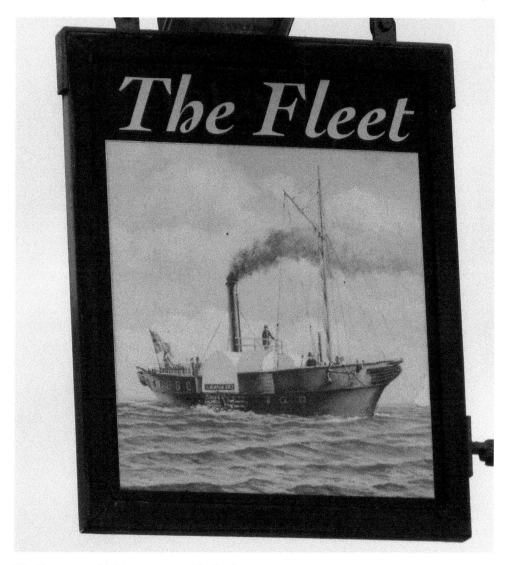

The Fleet sign, which is still up outside the flats.

multiple-occupation house was lodged with North Tyneside Council. It proposed that the now closed pub would have seven bedrooms, all with en-suite facilities, on the ground floor and six bedrooms (again, with en-suite facilities) on the first floor. A common kitchen and living room would also be on the first floor.

31. Aquatic Arms

It's hard to believe that this was once the Aquatic Arms. William George Rowntree was a beer retailer at No. 1 William Street in 1864 and when Jane Graham took over she was simply a beerhouse keeper. Robert Henderson first called it the Aquatic Arms in 1873. On 30 April 1892 the Calithumpian Quoit Club held their annual dinner at the inn, after which the winner of the Easter Handicap, Mr R, Dogherty, was presented with a Meerachaum pipe and a walking stick. Mr K. Fatten, who came second, received a handsome medal. On Tuesday 14 October 1890 the Tyne Volunteers Division Royal Engineers' Band was given supper by Mr and Mrs Hopkins on their celebrating their silver wedding anniversary. After supper the rest of the evening was spent in an entertaining manner. At the Brewster Sessions held for the Borough of Tynemouth on Friday 23 August 1895 Robert Turnbull, the tenant, was up before the magistrates to renew his licence, which had been objected to by a Mr Adamson on the grounds he had been convicted on 9 July for using the premises for betting. After deliberation the mayor decided to grant the application and renew the licence. On Thursday 12 March 1904 Robert was once again before the bench. This time the police were objecting to his licence being renewed on general grounds. Robert Turnbull was claiming an 1869 licence. After fifty-five minutes the bench decided to renew the licence on conditions laid down. On Friday 7 June 1935 interviews were held on the premises by the merchandise manager of International Trade Company, which required three additional sales representatives for the district of North Shields. Other firms with vacancies also used the premises for interviews; Mr Smith, whom I presume to be the manager, was the contact. On 4 February 1938 the Aquatic Arms music and singing

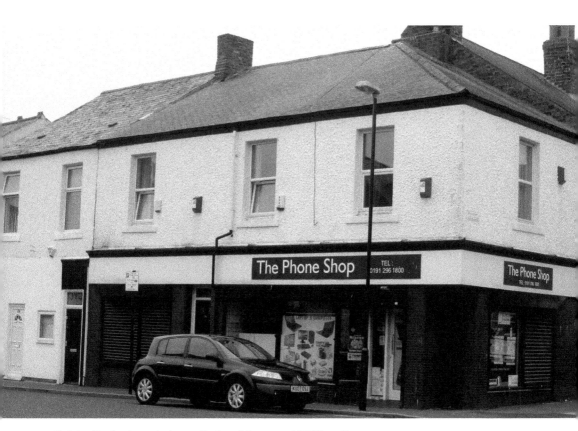

Originally the Aquatic Arms, Rudyerd Street and William Street.

licence was granted by Tynemouth Brewster Sessions. Already having a darts league in the town, in January 1950 a notice in the *Shields Daily News* informed all interested in a women's league to attend the Aquatic Arms on Thursday 26 January. The Aquatic Arms closed in the 1970s.

32. Neville Hotel

Alexander Barrass advertised the Neville Hotel in 1865 as being in Railway Street, but in the Ward's 1865/6 directory the address is Railway Terrace. On 7 January 1869 the hotel was up for let, and Harry Raynor became the new licensee. On Wednesday 21 April 1886 the illustrious members of Order of the Knights of Malta, after all the formalities, were over the members elected their new officers. On Monday 18 March 1889 the annual meeting of the North Shields Cycling Club was held at the hotel – the members totalled twenty-five. On 11 October 1895 the borough of Tynemouth Cricket Club held their forty-ninth annual meeting at the hotel, which was well attended. The year 1961 was the end of an era. Three barrels that had each held 60 gallons of spirit were removed from the hotel. These barrels, which had dominated the bar for as long as anyone could remember, were thought to be at least 100 years old and were the last of their kind in the town. At 7.30 on 7 November 1980 the North Tyneside branch of the Northumberland Hussars Association held their meeting at the hotel. The Neville Hotel is now housing.

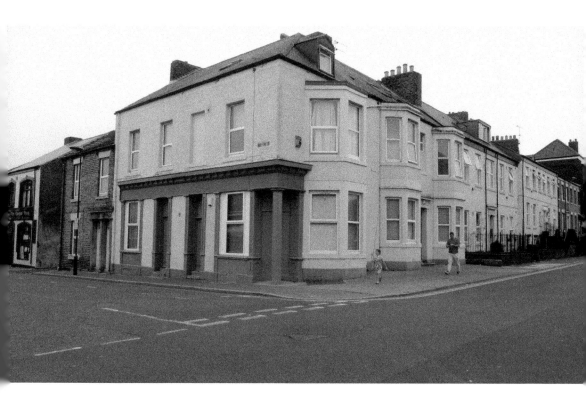

The Neville Hotel, Rudyerd Street and Railway Terrace.

33. European and United States Hotel

Patrick Duffy first called Nos 5 and 6 Railway Street the Spirit Vaults. In the *Newcastle Daily Chronicle*, on 7 July 1860, Mr Duffy advertised a 'New Hotel'. It was the European and United States Hotel, which he described as having excellent accommodation for families and visitors. On 12 September 1861 the European and United States Hotel was up for auction after Patrick Duffy's death. The hotel was described as consisting of numerous 'aired bedrooms, commercial and sitting room, good bar, bar parlour, coffee room, kitchen and a very spacious cellar. The out-offices are commensurate with the requirements of a hotel'. The *Newcastle Daily Chronicle*, on 28 November, announced Mrs Duffy had purchased the hotel and reopened it. When Mrs Mary M. Duffy advertised the hotel in 1865, she gave the address as the Market Place. On 7 May 1868 Thomas Mathison entered the hotel, announcing it had been put into such a state of order, comfort and convenience it would ensure the best entertainment and prompt attendance, with moderate charges. On 3 August 1876 Robert Humphrey, the licensee, was declared bankrupt. John Forster became the licensee until James William Newton became the new one in 1883. In 1893 it is simply called the European and in 1895 it is the European States, keeping that name until 1905 when it reverted back to being the European and United States. Later it became the County Hotel before being demolished possibly for the regeneration of the town centre.

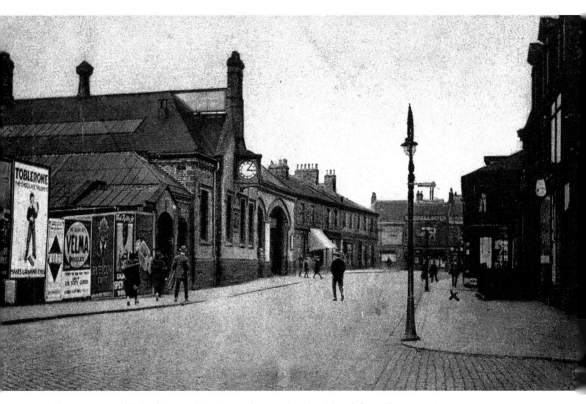

European and United States Hotel stood opposite the side of the railway station entrance.

34. Telegraph Hotel

Standing opposite the railway station, Mrs Jane Elliott advertised the Telegraph as a hotel at No. 2 Nile Street in 1859. John W. Thompson was the landlord in 1865, but in Ward's directory of 1865/6, J. Darling had become the landlord. On

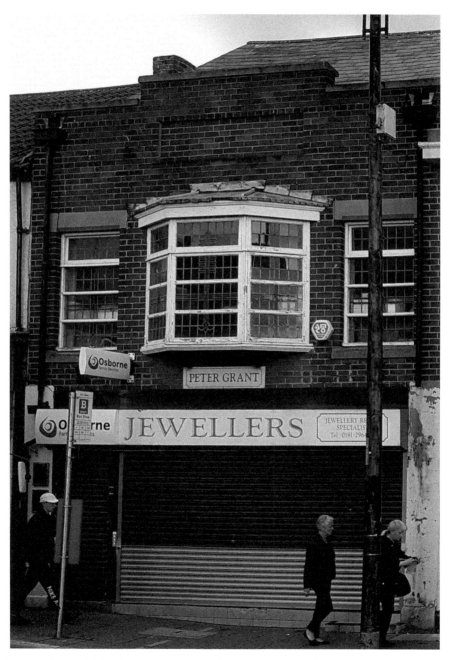

The Telegraph Hotel, Nile Street, stands opposite the entrance to the metro station.

Friday 2 March 1866 all the household furnishings of the hotel's eight apartments were sold by auction, including carpets, table cutlery, German silver goods, a few books and other sundries. When Thomas Eltringham became the landlord in September 1867 he informed the locals by advertising his intention of keeping it first class and hoped for a share of public patronage. In November 1942 before the Licensing Justices the licence of the hotel was transferred form Arnold Raine to Thomas Littlefair, the owner. No objections were offered by Mr Raine and the transfer was approved. On 17 April 1951 the inn was transferred from the previous owners J. G. Tuck and Son to the amalgamated firms of George Younger and Co. Ltd and R. Fenwick and Co. Ltd of Sunderland. On 20 January 1954 the *Telegraph* Inn B darts team won the Westoe Breweries Cup when they defeated the Black Bull Howdon in the final. On 10 December 1958 the inn held the presentation for the winners of the darts Tudor Cup. On 5 August 1962 a mystery blaze destroyed the storeroom at the inn, which had been locked and not used for years. Luckily the blaze did not disrupt the inn's activities. The Telegraph closed at the end of the 1960s to become a shop.

35. Railway Inn

In William's directory of 1844, John Gibbon advertised the Railway Inn, Little Bedford Street, as an 'Inn and Commercial Hotel'. 'J.G. can assure the public, that no expense shall be spared in making a Selection of Wines and Spirits, of the choicest Importation; and which he supplies at the *lowest possible Price.* To Commercial Men visiting Shields, his House will be found to embrace every Domestic Comfort that can be desired.' Omnibuses also ran from the inn for Tynemouth after every train, and there was one to convey passengers to any other part of the neighbourhood. On Monday 31 March 1845, the Railway Tavern (the premises of Mrs Gibson) was broken into. The lower part of the house was ransacked and a quantity of silver and German silver spoons stolen among other things. In July Michael Cawthorpe and Francis Cragg were charged with stealing a silver spoon the property of Jane Gibbon of the 'Railway Tavern Inn', Cawthorne was found guilty and given three months imprisonment to hard labour and one week each month in solitary. Then at the end of July John Waddles was charged with the stealing of a quantity of silver and other spoons from Mrs Gibbon. John Warddles was already serving a sentence in Durham Jail and when found guilty he was given transportation for ten years. In Slater's directory of 1846 there is a Railway Hotel licensee George Rowell and a Railway Inn licensee Jane Gibson both in Little Bedford Street. In 1850 George Rowell was still at the hotel, Robert Morton was licensee at the inn, by 1853 William Weatherill was advertising the Railway Inn and Posting House in Little Bedford Street, the hotel was in the hands of John Montgomery. William Weatherill first advertised the Railway Inn as being in Nile Street in 1859. In 1872 William Taylor advertised the inn as also having a Billiard Rooms. On Tuesday 18 April 1950 the hotel was allowed to have 'mechanical music' and supervised

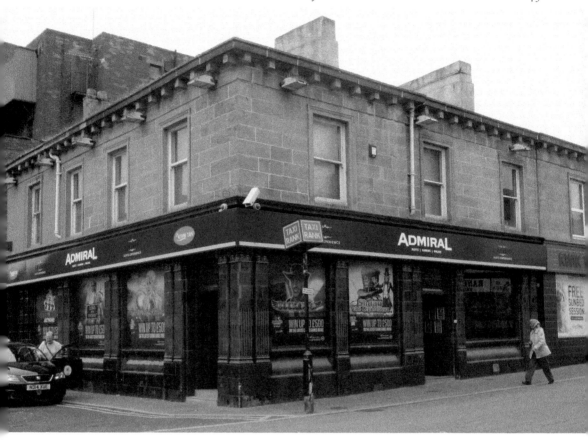

Railway Hotel, Nile Street.

concerts due to the granting a music and singing licence for all its public rooms with permission for alterations to be carried out on the premises. Today the inn is used as an amusement arcade.

36. Royal Arms

George Skipsey advertised the Royal Arms Hotel at No. 49 Nile Street in 1850. In 1854 John B. Barker was the landlord. On Monday 20 December 1857 the members of St Cuthbert's Church Choir held their supper at the hotel, this being a mark of approval from their respected pastor, Revenant Thomas Gillow. A meeting of the Royal Antediluvian Order of Buffaloes held their meeting at the hotel in May 1888. County Councillor Eskdale presided over one of the most successful smokers held by the North Shields Bicycle Club on 1 December 1891. The attendance was so large several were unable to enter the room. On Saturday 31 August 1895 a smoke concert was held for the National Order of Free Gardeners, which was well attended. Several of the grand officers attended, at which the Grand Master wore the splendid gold

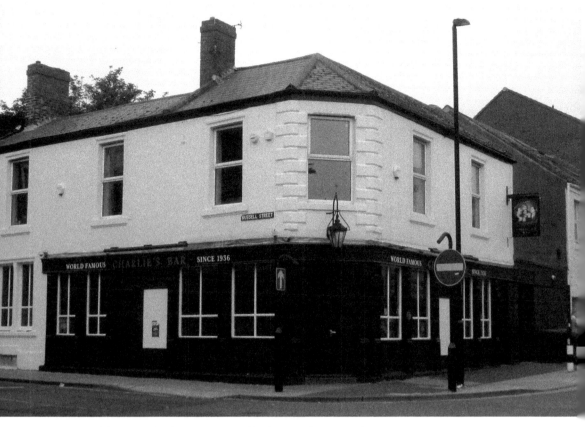

The world-famous Charlie's Bar, originally the Royal Arms, Nile Street.

chain that had been presented to the order by the mayor of Wolverhampton. On Saturday 12 January 1901 the Percy Main section of the Blyth and Tyne NER engine drivers, firemen and mineral guards held their annual dinner at the hotel. Lance Garrett catered for more than 100 guests who sat down to dinner. An interesting gathering of the Free Gardeners was held at the hotel on 12 April 1905. The initiation of several gentlemen as honorary members, including Mr Herbert Craig (prospective Liberal-Labour candidate for the borough), Councillor James Robinson, Mr C. G. Green, and Mr S. L. Robson took place. It is still open today as Charlie's Bar.

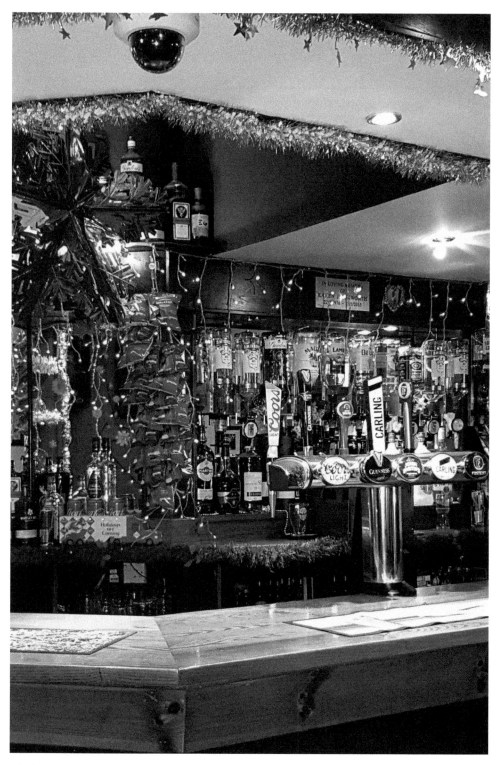

The bar stocks a selection of beer, wine and spirits.

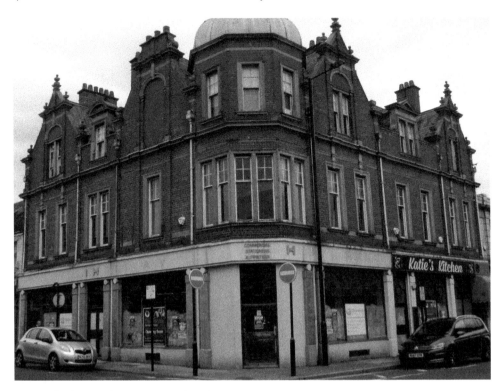

Originally the North Eastern Hotel, Nile Street.

37. North Eastern Hotel

Patrick Duffy advertised the original building on this site as the Spirit and Dublin Porter Vaults at No. 42 Nile Street in 1846. In 1850 Patrick Duffy describes himself as an ale, wine, and spirit merchant. In 1859 Edward Flinn now had No. 13$^{1}/_{2}$ West Percy Street as a Spirit Vault. When Thomas Flinn became the licensee in 1873 it had become the North Eastern Hotel at Nos 13–14 West Percy Street. Thomas died in 1874 leaving his wife Mary Jane Flinn to take over the hotel. In 1879 Mary Flinn is listed at 'Spirit Vaults', Nos 13, 14 and 15 West Percy Street. In 1883 Mary is still at the Spirit Vaults when she married John Stockton Rogers, where they stayed. In 1893 Mrs Mary J. Rodgers called the hotel Flinns. In 1895 Edward Fry Wood had become the new licensee and it was once again the North Eastern Hotel. By 1900 Robert Henderson of Westoe Breweries, South Shields, was the owner of the hotel, who described it as having a fully licensed restaurant and music room. In 1909 Joseph Johnson (Durham) Ltd bought the hotel. John Sutherland was the manager when it closed in 1964.

38. Spring Gardens

The original Spring Garden Inn on Albion Road West was built more than 250 years ago and known as the Flower Pot Inn. This old coaching inn was possibly the first calling point as the coaches made their way north and west from North Shields. In the early days the inn stood within a large garden that had a large pond stocked with goldfish. In 1822 Joseph Grey gave the address as Spring Gardens. In 1854 Joseph, who was now a victualler as well as a gardener, changed the name to the Spring Gardens Inn, Albion Road. In 1858 William Coxon became the licensee, giving the address as South Preston. William did not stay long as in 1861 Thomas Tynemouth was in residence. Thomas stayed twelve years then William Thompson, another market gardener, became the licensee. On Saturday 21 July 1884 a brass band contest was held in the field behind the inn, but unfortunately the weather was inclement and few spectators attended. Out of the eight bands entered only six turned up: Hebburn Colliery Band, The Tynemouth Artillery Band, the Newfield Band, Consett Ironworks Band, Tanfield Lea Band and the Ashington Band. It was in this order that the entertainment began. The inn was rebuilt in the 1933 by Newcastle Breweries Ltd when the new inn was to lose 140 square yards of land to the front for the widening of Albion Road. In June 1997, to commemorate seventy years of Newcastle Brown Ale, Newcastle Brewery chiefs unveiled the inn as the James H. Porter – after Colonel James H. Porter who first made the famous tipple in 1927. At the same time a limited number of bottles of Brown Ale featured Colonel Porter's picture, hoping that they would become a collector's item, and the money raised went to Tyneside charities. The public house is still open today.

Spring Gardens was originally called the Flower Pot Inn, an old coaching inn built over 250 years ago.

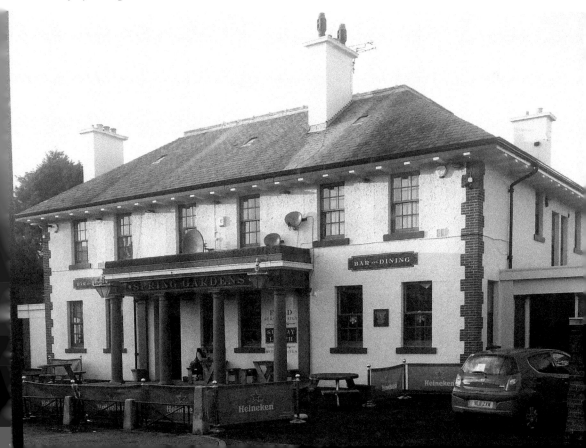

39. The Top House

According to the 1851 census Robert Davison Jackson was an innkeeper in Albion Street. In the 1853 North of England Directories Robert gave the address as No. 30 Nile Street and in Ward's 1875–76 directory Robert is listed as having a spirit bar. When Robert died in 1876 his wife Dorothy became the licence holder. In 1881 William Hedley was innkeeper. When William died his wife Ann took over the inn and renamed it the Albion, where she stayed until the end of 1884. Thomas Mothersdale placed an advert in the *Shields Daily News* on 24 December 1885 announcing that he had taken over the inn, which had undergone repairs and made most comfortable. A supply of wines and spirits of the best quality were available, and every comfort was available for his guests. On 22 July 1941 at the transfer sessions of the Tynemouth Borough Licensing Justices, the bench allowed the transfer of the licence form Mr Bertram Richard Lloyd, who had joined the army, to Mr R. Chisholm. In more recent times it has become known as the Top House.

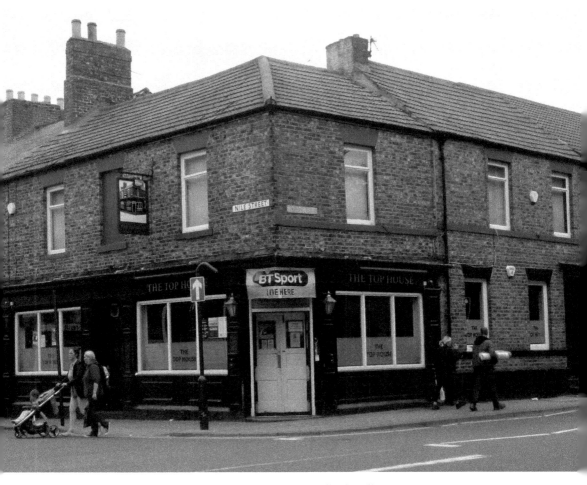

The Top House, Nile Street and Albion Road – originally the Albion Inn.

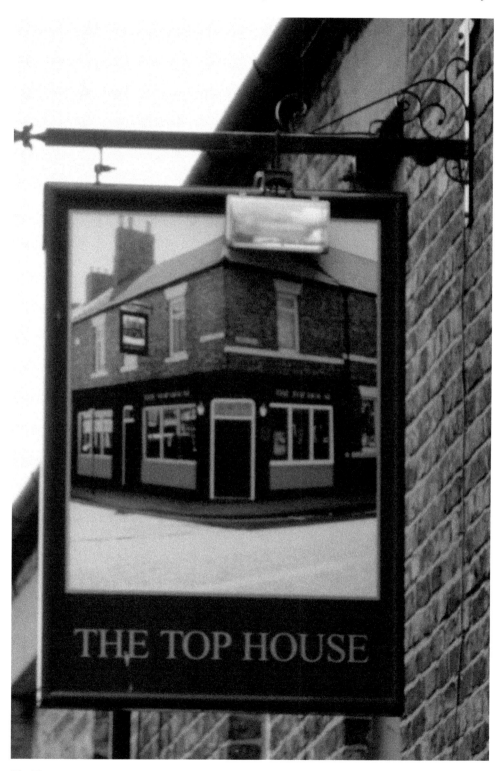

The Top House sign.

40. Old Hundreds Inn

On Tuesday 25 January 1842 the Independent Order of Oddfellows, Manchester Unit, opened the Prince of Wales Lodge in the Victoria Inn when a number of respectable individuals were initiated as members. James Sims advertised the Victoria Tavern in 1844 and the address was No. 100 Church Way, and on Wednesday 2 July 1845 an auction was held there. By 1846 Ann Murray had become the licensee. In 1857 when Jane Swan Thompson was licensee she gave the address as No. 69 Church Way. John Short is listed as licensee in Ward's 1865/6 directory, and on 9 November 1865 the whole of the household furniture and bar fittings of John Short were to be auctioned as he was leaving the business. Robert Potts then became the licensee. In 1886 Robert Pott, wine and spirit merchant, called the inn the Old Hundreds Inn. In August 1894 Mr J. C. Dury, draper of Alma Place, placed an objection to the licence of the Old Hundreds, as it was now known, because of its proximity to Royal Jubilee School and liquor was being served on the Albion Street side, which was not licensed. Robert Potts had not sold liquor there, but when Farquhar Deuchar of Deuchar Ltd took over the tavern a long bar was installed along with two drinking rooms in that section, which at one time had been the Angel Inn. Mr Potts' sister had bought the premises in 1865. When finding doors that had been between Albion Road and Church Way bricked up, he pulled the obstruction down in 1866. Several people admitted drinking there over the last fifteen years. Mr Eskdale did not attend court to give evidence, so the case was dismissed. On Wednesday 2 September 1992 the *Evening Chronicle* featured British Brewery Month and was giving away 3,000 pints

Victoria Hotel, better known as the old Hundreds, Church Way.

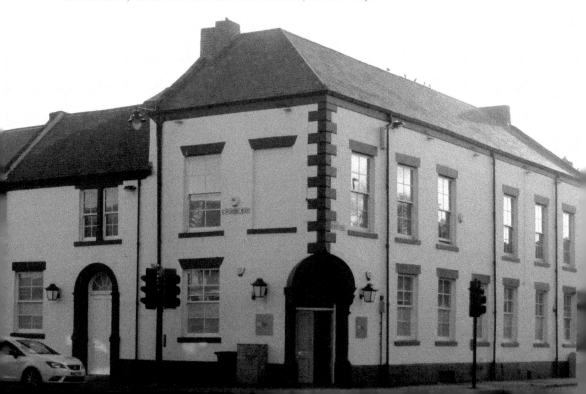

of Newcastle Exhibition, with the Old Hundreds its feature pub. The vouchers in the paper were to be handed over after 8 p.m. that day and the first 100 people would receive a free pint. Ye Old Hundreds, as it became known, had a celebratory 100th birthday party on 21 August 1994 when Jackie Grady and Steve Yeats had a pie and pea supper and staged a Victorian fancy dress competition. Beer had also been reduced to £1 a pint. After changing names several times, the latest being the Tun, it is no longer a public house.

41. Queen's Head

Originally the Queen's Head when advertised by Archibald Hunter in 1821. When Archibald died his wife Sarah became the licensee in 1827 and gave the address as Turnpike Road. On Tuesday 6 September 1831 a third part or share was sold at auction at the Albion Hotel. It was described as being in the very best and most central part of the town, with stables and yard attached and capable of taking eight horses. William Weatherilt became the proprietor. In 1834 he gave the address as No. 8 Albion Street. In 1853 William Weatherilt Sr advertised the Queen's as an inn and posting house. In 1854 William Cummings White became the licensee. When the inn came up for auction on Tuesday 18 February 1866, while in the occupation of George Thompson, the ground floor comprised a parlour, taproom, bar, and small sitting room; the first floor comprised a dining room and bedroom; and the basement held a capital beer cellar and useful kitchen. It was closed in 2010 and reopened just before Christmas 2012 as the Pub and Kitchen by brother and sister Paul Bell and Denise Davies.

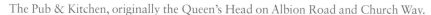

The Pub & Kitchen, originally the Queen's Head on Albion Road and Church Way.

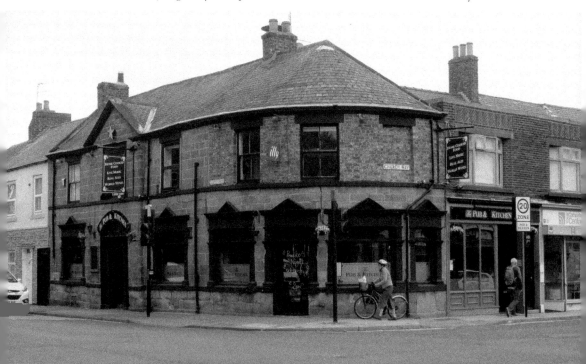

42. Oddfellows

At the Brewster Sessions held on 22 September 1868 Matthew Gillespie was applying for a licence for his premises in Gray Street, which is not far from where the Oddfellows now stands. In 1869 he is described as a beer retailer and gave the address as Coburg Street. In 1875–76 Robert Brewis is described as a beer retailer at No. 56 Grey Street, and by 1879 John Grey was the beer retailer here. John is still advertising as a beer retailer in Kelly's directory of 1886, but on 10 March 1886, when John Gray died, the Oddfellows Arms was his address. On 11 March 1886 the Independent Order of Oddfellows Kingston Unity, Blyth and Tyne district, 'Duke of Wellington Lodge', was invited to the funeral of Brother John Gray on Sunday 14 March. John's wife Christine took over the running of the inn. On 10 November 1908 a presentation was held for Mr John Potts, who was connected with the fishing industry and was leaving Shields to go to West Africa in connection with the fishing industry there. Mr A. Robson presented him with a silver mounted pipe in a case. On 20 September 1938 the licence of the Oddfellows was transferred from William Percy Forster to Christopher Railton Patterson who was leaving the Ship Inn, Middle Street. In March 1940 Christopher Patterson was granted a wine licence by Tynemouth Licensing Commission upgrading the arms from beer only. On 20 July 1953 the magistrates at Tynemouth Licensing Sessions gave permission to carry out structural alterations on the inn in Grey Street. In January 1954 the Oddfellows was granted a music and singing licence for the sitting room. The Oddfellows moved to their new premises in the 1980s where in July 1999

The Oddfellows Arms, Albion Road.

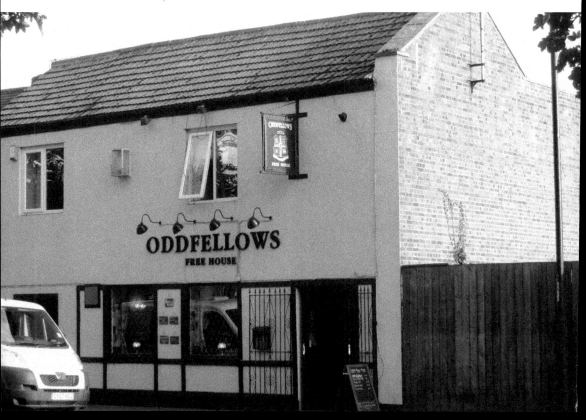

an application was made to convert the first-floor function room into a self-contained flat. In May 2002 the Oddfellows was up for sale, priced £150,000, as the present owners were retiring after thirteen years. The Oddfellows is still open today.

43. Artillery Arms

Jeera Tandoori on Albion Road was originally the Three Bull's Head when advertised in 1827 by Ann Spittal and then the Artillery Arms, which according to the licencing register had been a beerhouse since 1867. In 1883 Charles Spooner was the manager. On 13 March 1897 after thirty years at the Skinners Arms Inn, Gilesgate, Hexham, Mrs White became the new licensee. Ralph Pringle, the licensee in July 1912, was summoned before Tynemouth Borough Court, being charged with keeping a dangerous dog. An order was made to keep the dog under control and he had to pay costs. James Henry Tuck was granted permission to alter the Artillery in November 1944 by removing a partition wall upstairs to make a room for both men and women as there was a lavatory for women upstairs. He would then bar women from the downstairs sitting room. In March 1949 James Henry Tuck was granted a full licence enabling the sale of spirits. The Artillery closed in the 1960s.

Jeera Tandoori was once the Artillery Arms, Albion Road.

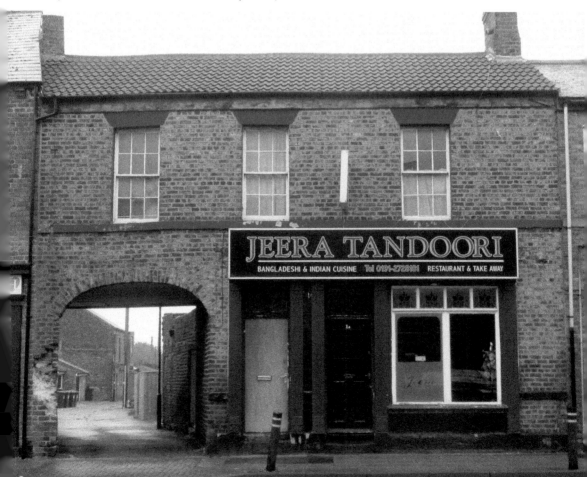

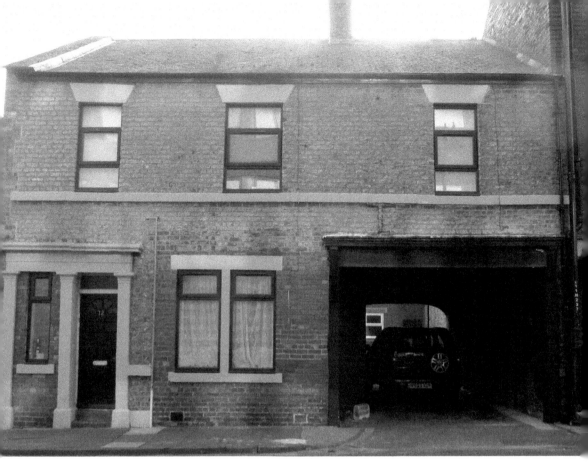

The Golden Fleece Inn, Norfolk Street

44. Golden Fleece

When William Armstrong advertised in the North of England Directory of 1853 this was called the Norfolk Arms. In 1854 Edward Hogg was the landlord, but when Robert William Wade became the landlord in 1861 the name had changed and it became known as the Golden Fleece. In the *Shields Daily News* on Monday 15 August 1870 the inn was up for sale by 'Private Contract' and was described as containing eight rooms, a large cellar, and a splendid bar entrance from two streets. Applications were to be made to Mr Dawson on the premises. James G. Clark became the licensee. In August 1875 the inn was once again up for auction at the Albion Hotel. It was described as 'an inn and spirit bar' with a price set at £700. It was sold at £1,500 – a considerable sum in those days. On 5 April 1881 when John Forster moved to the inn he put a notice in the *Shields Daily News* informing his friends that he had moved there from the European Hotel with a stock of Bass's ales, wines and spirits on offer. On 22 May 1888 George Willis, joiner, tobacconist and licensed victualler of Low Street and the Golden Fleece, was before the Newcastle Bankruptcy Court. Mr Willis owed unsecured creditors £315 3s 11d, with assets of only £69 2s 11d. He attributed his insolvency to bad trade and heavy expenditure.

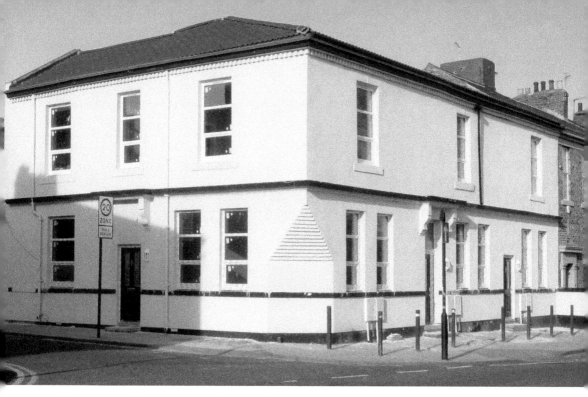

Victoria Inn, Albert Terrace and North Church Street.

45. Victoria Inn

In 1871 William Prince was the licensee of the Victoria Inn. The address was No. 1 Albert Terrace. By 1873 Mrs Mary H. Davis had taken over the inn and the address was No. 1 Albert Terrace and North Church Street. When Robert Park took over in 1875 the address was No. 1 Church Street. On 25 April 1934 proposed plans for alterations to the Victoria Hotel on the corner of Church Street and Tynemouth Road were submitted by A. Pearson for J. W. Cameron. Councillor William Little was licensee of the hotel in 1953 and was made mayor that year; he had declined becoming mayor the year before. On 10 April 1954 Mr and Mrs K. Brown announced that the hotel had been granted a full licence – it had previously only had a beer licence. In the late 1980s the hotel became known as the Tap and Spile with the hope that it would revive the inn. In January 1991 the manager Rob Barraclough, selling as many as ten guest beers, scooped the Pub of the Year Award from CAMRA (Campaign for Real Ale). The Victoria was converted into flats in 2019.

46. Albert Inn

In 1861 William Moore was a grocer at No. 19 Albert Terrace. In 1867 William was an innkeeper and in 1871 William was advertising the property as the Albert Inn, with the address changing over the years between Albert Terrace and No. 1 North King Street. William stayed at the inn until 1886 when Charles Dunn became the licensee. By 1900 Robert Henderson of Westoe Brewery, South Shields, was the owner of the inn and in 1905 Robert Henderson Jr was the licensee. By 1909 Joseph Johnson (Durham Ltd)

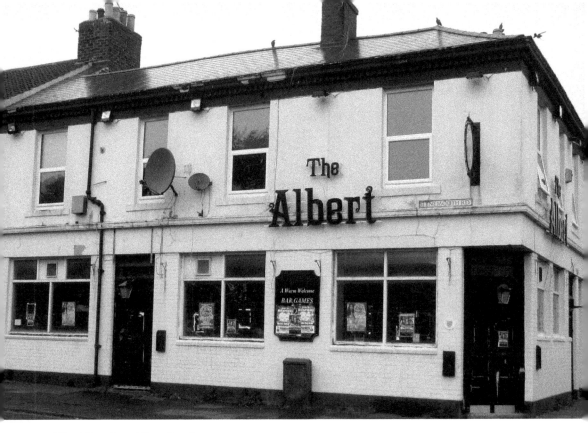

The Albert Inn, Albert Road.

was the new owner, keeping the inn until 1938 when John Southern became the new owner. On 20 September 1938, on the third attempt, Tynemouth Licensing Magistrates granted permission for structural alterations, which would mean making the select room and the sitting room into one large lounge. On 7 June 1949 Tynemouth Licensing Magistrates granted the transfer of the singing and dancing licence from John Sutherland Sr (deceased) to John Sutherland Jr. The Albert closed in 2012 and in 2019 was converted into a shop.

47. The Langley Castle

The Langley Castle Inn was advertised in Ward's directory of 1859/6 by Isaac Ridley Robson, giving the address as Tynemouth Road. On 15 October 1860 the inn, a free and well-accustomed freehold public house, was up for auction – at this time still in the occupation of Isaac Ridley Robson. The house was described as containing 'a tap room, bar parlour, and bar on the ground floor; with a good kitchen, pantry and cellarage in the basement. On the first floor the long room was about 21 feet by 16, and a good bedroom: also two bedrooms above each with a fire place. A large yard, with every convenience, at the rear of the house, a flower garden, with metal pallisading(sic) in front.' 'Substantially built with all the sanitary requirements of the Local Board of Health, also with all modern improvements necessary for the carrying on the sale of ale, wine and spirits.' In 1865 when James Scott, a licensed victualler,

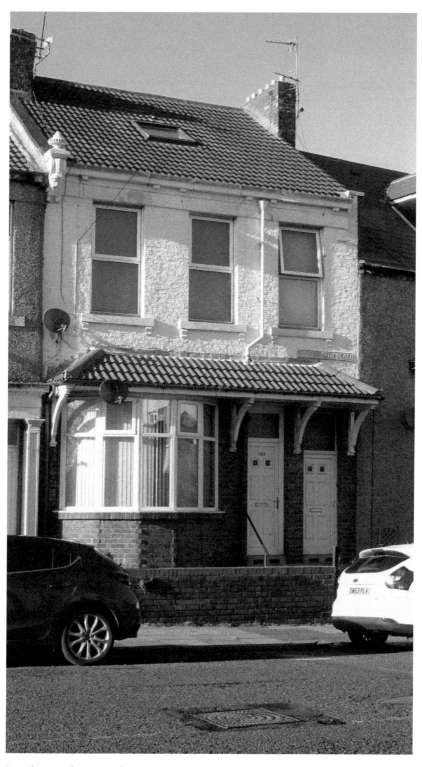

Langley Castle Inn, Coburg Terrace.

advertised the inn the address was No. 11 Cobourg Terrace. On Tuesday 3 May 1887 Mr Robert Morrison Tate offered for sale several properties situated in North Shields, in accordance with on order from the High Court of Justice, Chancery Division, which included the Langley Castle. It began at £500 and was withdrawn at £910. In 1893 Andrew Nichol Dodds acquired the inn, selling it to W. B. Reid & Co. Ltd in 1920. They sold the inn for housing in 1935.

48. Coburg Inn

Plans for a new hotel to be built on the Tynemouth Lodge estate were passed by Tynemouth Council on 28 July 1869. The new hotel was the Coburg and it was listed in 1871 as being at No. 12 Coburg Terrace. On Tuesday 14 October 1873 at the Albion Hotel, Norfolk Street, the Coburg was being auctioned by Mr Jackson. After a brisk bidding it was purchased by Mr Wilkie for £4,025. In April 1984 Jim and Emily Johnston, licensees of the hotel, had decided to leave as trade had deteriorated since they had taken over four years previously. Stating the lack of work and the Fish Quay being non-existent, people were not going in until 9.30 p.m., which was hitting the trade hard. In May that year regulars at the pub organised a darts marathon, raffles

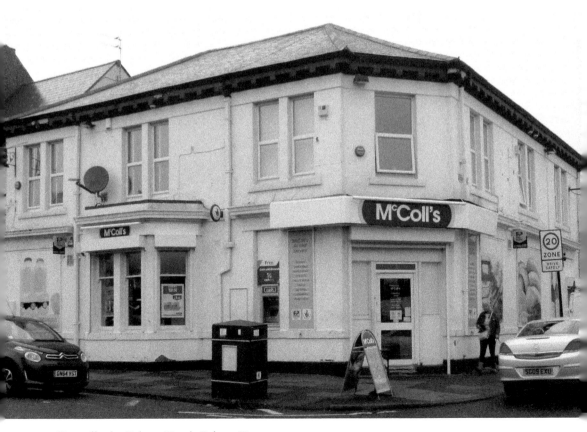

Formally the Coburg Hotel, Coburg Terrace.

and other events and raised £630 for the Cavitron Laser Appeal and Cathy Secker, TV announcer, handed over the money to neurosurgeon Mr R. M. Kalbag of Newcastle General Hospital on their behalf. In February 1992 the Coburg closed for a complete refit. When Vaux reopened the public house not only been completely refurbished but also had a new name and a new licensee. Malcolm Readman an ex-fireman had chosen the name 'The Mash Tun'. The pub was certainly everything the old Coburg had not been; it was now a fashionable one-room pub instead of having several smaller ones, and it had a different outlook and atmosphere as well. Unfortunately it did not last and in 2007 it closed.

49. Tynemouth Lodge

When William Tate advertised the Tynemouth Lodge Hotel in 1821 the address was simply Tynemouth Road. The plaque on the wall states the building has been in use as a hotel and public house since 1799. Situated next door is the former house of correction, a prison for minor offenders. A tunnel runs between the cellar kitchen in the lodge and the correction house, which allowed meals to be taken into the house to the justice and inmates. On Tuesday 24 May 1803 a meeting was held at the hotel for the members of the late North Shields and Tynemouth Volunteers, gentleman

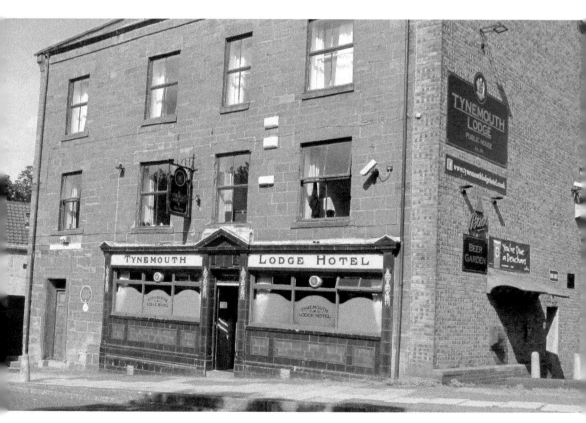

Tynemouth Lodge Hotel, Tynemouth Road.

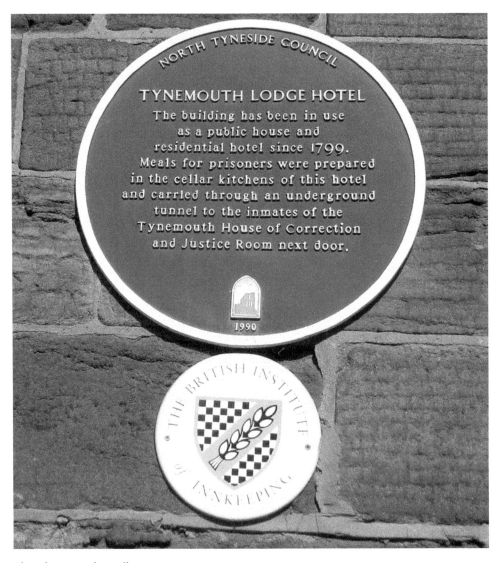

NORTH TYNESIDE COUNCIL

TYNEMOUTH LODGE HOTEL
The building has been in use
as a public house and
residential hotel since 1799.
Meals for prisoners were prepared
in the cellar kitchens of this hotel
and carried through an underground
tunnel to the inmates of the
Tynemouth House of Correction
and Justice Room next door.

1990

THE BRITISH INSTITUTE OF INNKEEPING

Blue plaque on the wall.

householders and others in the area having not previously belonged to the corps, for the purpose of offering their services to the government at the time of the present crisis (war with Napoleon). In June 1841 after the death of her husband Samuel, Ann Matthew put the lodge up to let, William Hooper became the licensee. At the end of December 1983 after being closed down and boarded up by the brewery Hugh Price, a real ale fan and a founder member of CAMRA, took on the hotel. He spent more than £40,000 on a facelift, giving it an old Victorian style and taking it back to the days when beer was drawn from the wood. Like most hotels of this age it also has at least one ghost: that of a lady who has been seen chasing young children. The hotel is still open today.

50. Dolphin Inn

When Ralph Hopper advertised the Dolphin in 1834 the address was simply Tynemouth. The Dolphin Inn has been on the same site for more than 400 years, although it was enlarged and remodelled in early 1934 by Messrs Archibald Arrol & Sons Ltd. The rooms had been laid out in a special design to give the bar area central control and supervision. There were several smaller rooms, including the gentlemen's smoking room, with small tables and chairs. The lounge had restful decorations in fawn, the ceiling had a panelled effect and there were small tables, chairs and seating around the walls, along with a fireplace of cut steel that was particularly striking. The lounge could be completely cut off during non-licence hours to provide meals and afternoon tea. In April 1984, the manager, Mr Gordon Robson, resigned stating that he was working 100 hours a week because of it being a way of life and you had to have a calling for that type of work. Marina Richards was the new landlady. By May 1994 the Dolphin had become known for its excellent meals being good value for money with steaks from 5oz to 32oz washed down with a pint of Marston's Pedigree, Burtons Ale, Tetley's bitter or larger. Today it still advertises two-course specials from Tuesday to Saturday.

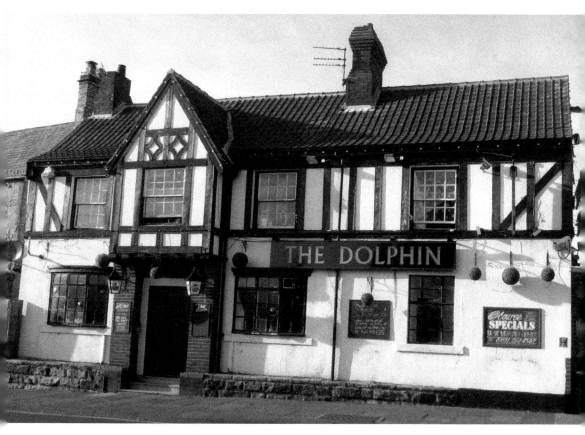

Dolphin Inn, King Edward Road, Tynemouth.

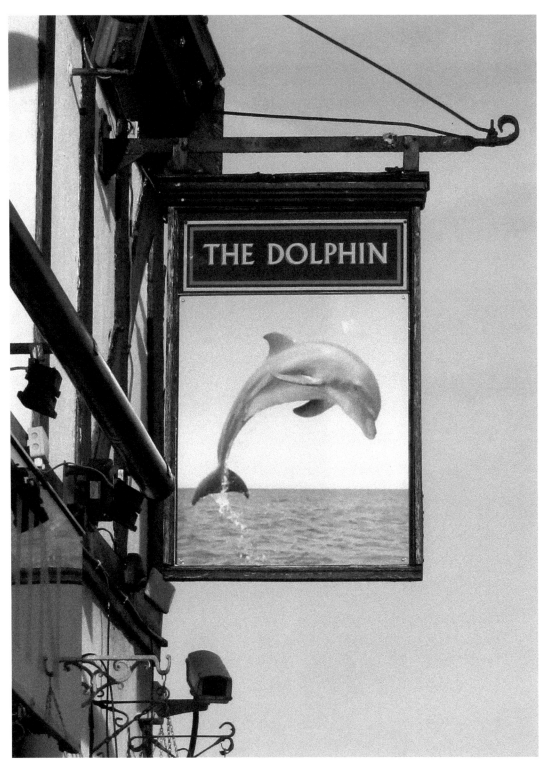

Dolphin sign.

51. Star & Garter

This large Georgian house, originally the Star and Garter Inn, was first heard about in the *Newcastle Courant* on 25 February 1803, advertising the sale of a freehold dwelling house to be sold on Tuesday 8 March. John Robinson, the licence holder, died at the inn on 20 December 1826 and John Tayler then became the licensee. On Tuesday 8 March 1831 the Port of Newcastle Association for the Preservation of Life From Shipwreck held a general meeting for subscribers to, and friends of, the association. After the meeting, a trial of the Manby Apparatus was held at Tynemouth Lifeboat Station. The kit belonged to Captain Dansey. In 1843 John Taylor made considerable alterations to the inn, with good accommodation, good stabling, lockup coach house and steady hostler. On Wednesday 16 July 1845 a party of friends of Misses F. and E. Archbold gave a welcome dinner for them to celebrate the opening of the 'Hotel', which had undergone extensive improvement. When William Newton moved into the hotel in April 1847 he announced all it's attributes, besides having good stabling he also said it was within two minutes of Tynemouth station on the Newcastle & Berwick

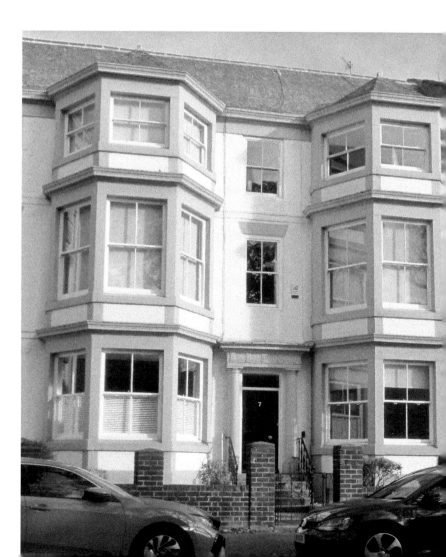

Star and
Garter Inn,
Manor Road.

Railway. On Thursday 7 October 1847 his friends gave him a welcome dinner; tickets were £1 1s and dinner was at four o'clock sharp. The inn was again advertised to let in November 1848 – with a very grand description – and Miss Maria MacGregor became the new licensee. In 1871 William Henry Scott, a merchant, was living at No. 7 Front Street, which gives the impression it was no longer a hotel.

52. Cumberland Arms

In 1841, Abigal Graham was a publican in Front Street, but it was not until 1846 that George Rogers advertised the Cumberland Arms Inn. His wife Jane became the licensee in 1854. On 21 February 1884 the landlord William Elsbury was charged with unlawfully selling a pint of ale to Daniel Murray on Sunday 17th while he was drunk. William was fined 10s and costs. In September 1884 the licensee William Flowry (sic) was blacklisted at Tynemouth Brewster Session for permitting drunkenness. On 24 August 1898, at the annual Brewster Sessions, Mr Bramwell applied on behalf of the owners for sanctions to pull down the Cumberland Arms and rebuild it. After consideration the application was refused. The material objection was the increase of

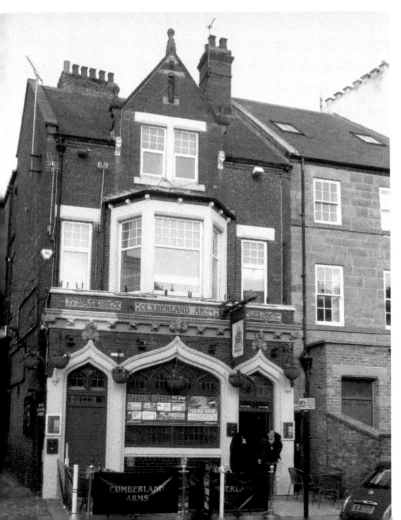

Cumberland Arms, Front Street, Tynemouth.

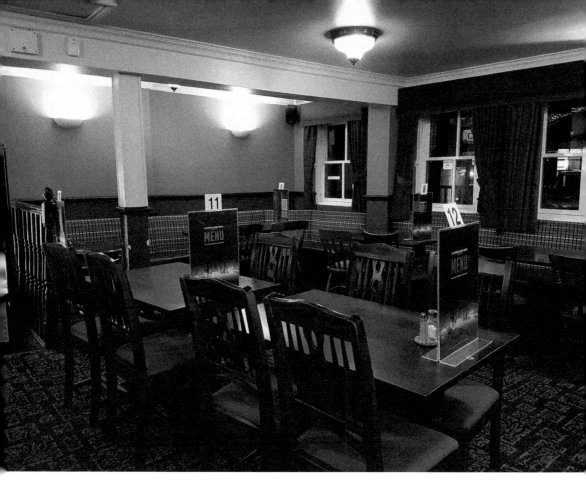

The dining area on the upper level of the Cumberland Arms.

the drinking facilities. At a special transfer session in June 1944 at the Police Court in North Shields Licensing Bench, the licence of the Cumberland Arms was transferred from the late Mrs Emily Nicholson to Mr Alfred Henry Smith. Newcastle Breweries awarded the inn with the best exterior award for its display between spring and summer of 1991. On Wednesday 3 June 1998, with landlord Dave Irving, the Cumberland Arms was known to have some of the best and cheapest prices on Tynemouth Front Street. Being a Scottish and Newcastle-managed house, it sold a selection of Theakston and McEwan's ales. The Cumberland Arms now sells real ales with two bars on split levels and, being family friendly, it also sells a range of meals – both lunch and evening – in its restaurant area.

53. Bath Hotel

This lovely five-storey building was the Bath Inn, Bath Terrace, when advertised by Hannah Spurrier in 1821. A subscription ball was held at the hotel on Tuesday 12 March 1844. Ladies' tickets were 5s and gentlemen's were 6 – including refreshments. Dancing commenced at nine o'clock. These balls attracted the elite of the district, who could afford the ticket price. On 9 October 1850 James Anderson placed a

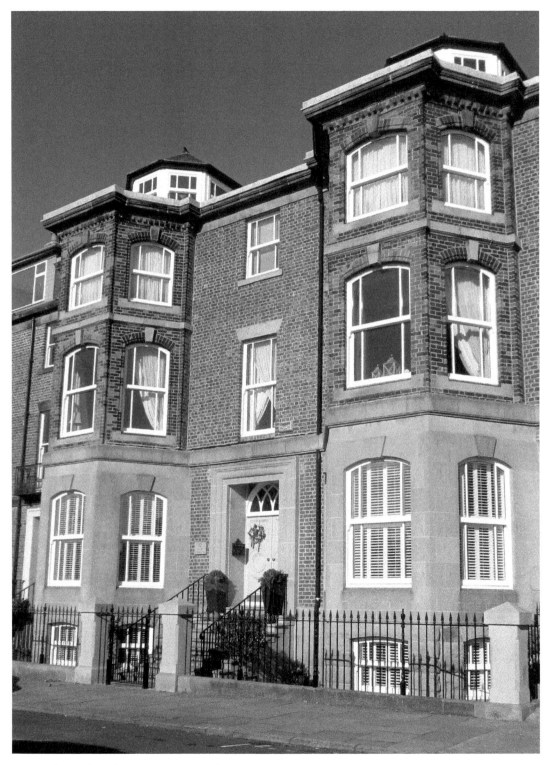

Bath Hotel, Bath Terrace, Tynemouth.

notice in the *Newcastle Courant* thanking his clientele for their patronage, which he had received over the past ten years he had occupied the hotel. James was moving to the Royal Hotel by Tynemouth railway station. On 11 December 1850 William Beaumont placed an advert in the *Newcastle Courant* announcing that he had entered the old, established, first-rate hotel and hoped he may merit a share of their patronage and support. Mr W. Sidney Gibson Esquire, FSA, gave a lecture on the history, architecture and antiquities of Tynemouth Priory on Friday 22 July 1853 in aid of funds for the preservation and repair of the ruins of the priory church. In July 1859 workmen started excavating the ground next to the hotel for the foundations of the new Assembly Rooms. Thursday 30 October saw the Manor of Bath Building Society hold their first general meeting at the 'inn' for the election of officers and to agree rules and other business. On Saturday 6 June 1891 a company called the Tynemouth Bath Hotel Co. Ltd was before Mr P. Stirling at the Local Law Cases of the Chancery Division. The petition before the court asked that they confirm resolutions adopted by the company for a reduction of their capital. The company formed to carry on a hotel business with a nominal capital of 150 shares of £100 each. Of these, 100 had been issued and £50 paid on each, with that they bought the hotel and borrowed £4,500 for working the business. The company had lost £3,500 by depreciation in the value of the furniture, the hotel property and other causes. What they then proposed was to convert the whole of the shares so as not to touch the credit of the company. His lordship made an order to the terms of the petition. The hotel reopened on 16 June 1891. On 8 December 1950 the Women's Committee of the Percy Park RFC held a dance at the hotel in which around 200 attended, with the proceeds going to the proposed new pavilion for the Preston Road ground. On 13 April 1958 fire swept through the hotel, damaging both the lounge and buffet bars, but Fredrick Bennington, manager, held business as usual, with clientele being served by candlelight at the temporary bar he had set up. Approval was granted in January 1959 for alterations to be carried out to increase the service facilities, but sadly the hotel is now a residential property.

54. Percy Arms

William Smith was the landlord of the Percy Arms when Robert Appleby held an auction there on Thursday 23 August 1832. Being auctioned was one moiety (half, part, portion or share) of the tythe of corn and grain left to the poor of the parish by the late Sir Ralph Milbank. In March 1838 the Duke of Northumberland put the inn up for let. It stated that it was intended the premises would need to undergo repairs to render it fit to continue as an inn, or occupied as one or two dwelling houses. Originally a three-storey building only occupying that part of the site where the door is, it underwent a complete rebuilt in 1931 to incorporate the shop on the corner. On 31 October 1991 James Ridley Sample applied for an entertainment licence, which would be from 11 a.m. to 11 p.m. for six days a week. In November 1994 Margaret Gales, the manager of the Percy Arms, was presented with the Metro Shields for winning the Floral Display Competition organised by the Tynemouth Village Association. In February 2005 David Elgie was the first landlord to apply

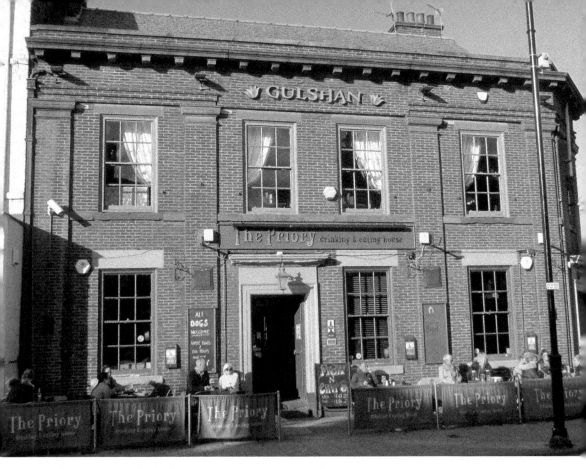

The Priory – originally the Percy Arms, Front Street, Tynemouth.

for a twenty-four-hour drinks licence, although he stated that he had no intention of opening round the clock. On 2 June 2005 soccer legend Jack Charlton held an evening talk, with the proceeds from the sale of tickets – £6 each – going to the Disabled Anglers Trust. In 2009, after being closed, it changed its name the Priory. A pub of that name – Priory Inn – was at one time situated beside the Gibraltar Rock in East Street.

55. Salutation Inn

An advert in the *Newcastle Courant* on 9 July 1757 was for a new 'Genteel Machine' for passengers. Starting on Monday 18 July, it would set off from the Boar's Head in Newcastle to the Sun in North Shields at seven o'clock, returning at 9. Then in the afternoons it set out for the Salutation and returned the same day. Fares from Shields were 1s, and from Tynemouth 1s 3d. On Sunday 2 March 1797 Thomas Sterling, master of the inn, died. In 1821 Elizabeth Scott was the licensee, and in 1834 Thomas Ferguson was the landlord. In May 1844 Mr Liddell held a two-hour lecture in the long room of Robert Mill's inn on the Corn Laws and strikes. On Thursday 13 July 1848, Titus Howett, licensee of the inn, held a sale of fine arts at one o'clock in the long room, which included watercolour and oil paintings, framed in gold and maple or gold

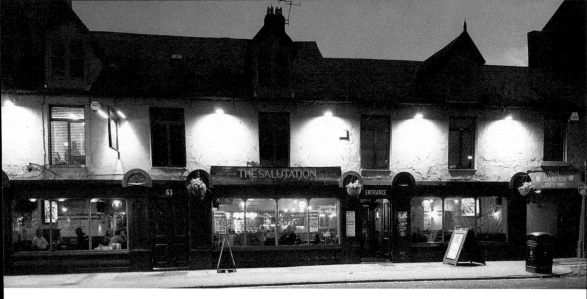

Above: Salutation Arms, Front Street, Tynemouth.

Below: The bar of the Salutation.

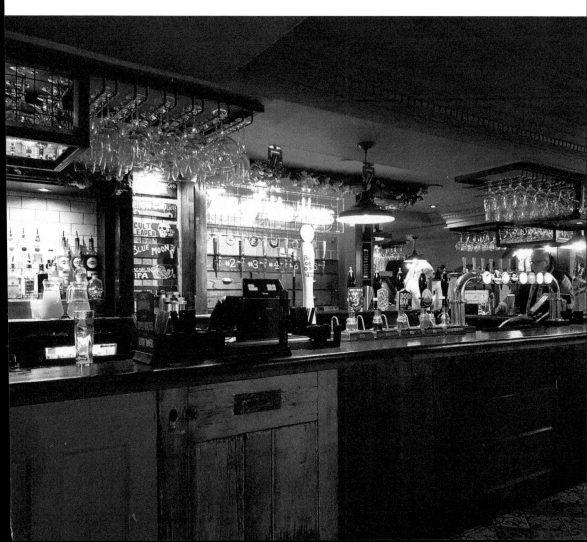

and oak. The Lockwood Family, a group of performers on the harp, gave a concert to a crowded fashionable audience in the long room on the evening of 23 January 1850. When in March 1874 William Foster left the inn all his household furniture was sold by auction on Monday 30 March at eleven o'clock. John Rutherford then became the licensee. When the inn came on the market at auction on Wednesday 15 May 1878 it was described as 'containing bar, two taprooms, smoke room, sitting room, club room, four bedrooms, three attics, kitchen, and cellar, with an extended range of stabling, coach house &c., at the rear and a shop and house with three rooms adjoining'. Bidding stated at £3,000 and the competition was brisk; Mr Scott of North Shields purchased it for £4,200. In May 1880 the 'hotel' was up for let. In May 1994 the newly refurbished inn was again reopened by Kerry and Geena Orrell, with a refurbished beer garden ready for the summer visitor.

56. Turk's Head

Henry Bolton advertised the Turk's Head in 1827, and on Monday 14 May 1827 the *Wellington Coach* was advertised as running from the Mr Bolton's inn from 8.15 a.m. every morning except Sunday. It went through Dockwray Square to Newcastle and left Mr Miller's Half Moon Inn at Big Market at 3.30 p.m., and Mr Richardson's Three Indian Kings, Quayside, at 4 p.m. every afternoon for Tynemouth. In February 1842 the members of the Loyal Tynemouth Castle Lodge of the Independent Order of Oddfellows, Manchester Unity, celebrated their first anniversary by having dinner at the inn now in the hands of Mr E. Johnson. On 8 March 1880 John Hunter, innkeeper of the inn, filed for liquidation at Newcastle Crown Court and Mr James Mallet was appointed receiver. In April 1882 a well-known dog called Wandering Willie died and Andrew Nichol Dodds had his hide preserved and placed in a case at the inn. Willie was a collie. In the early 1870s a shepherd from the Cheviots was taking his flock to the Cleveland Hills. On reaching the North Shields ferry he counted his sheep and found one missing, so sent Willie to find it. When the ferry approached upon recounting his flock they all were there, but Willie had not returned. Not wanting to miss the ferry he proceeded with the flock. Willie returned to find his master gone, so waited for him. When the master did not return he got on the ferry to follow, only his master was on one coming in the opposite direction, so they missed each other. Willie wandered around for some time and was eventually 'adopted' by a Ralph Cruickshanks, staying with him until he died. On 18 May 1897 Andrew Nichol Dodds made an application to the Tynemouth Licensing Committee held at North Shields Police Court for singing and music licences for the inn were granted. At a special meeting of the Tynemouth Licensing Committee an application was made for the transfer of the inn from Mr Andrew Nichol Dodds, deceased who had owned and managed it, to that of his son Mr William Dodds. The magistrates granted the transfer. The Turk's Head is still open today.

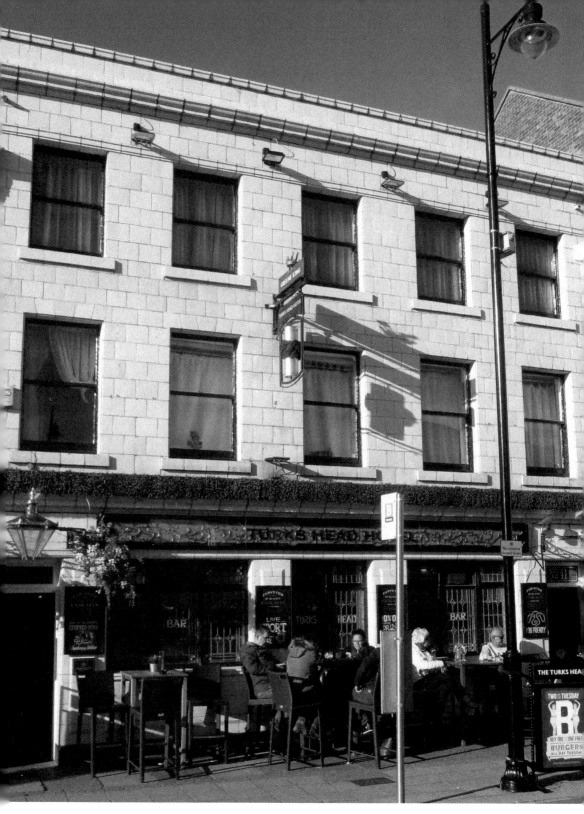

The Turk's Head, Front Street, Tynemouth.

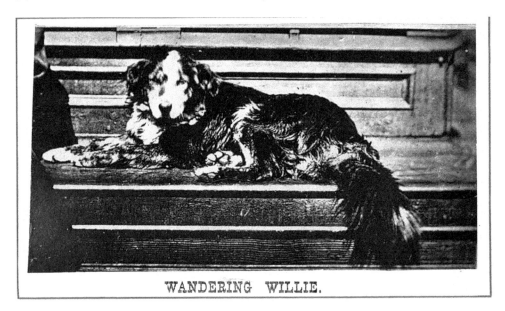

WANDERING WILLIE.

The legendary Wandering Willie once resided in a case in the Turk's Head.

57. Gibraltar Rock

Ann Scott advertised the Gibraltar Rock in 1827, but in December 1832 the inn, which stands with its back to the sea, was to be let and Mary Scott became the licensee, giving the address as No. 3 East Street. By 1846 Thomas Scott Thorpe had taken over the inn, and on his death on 28 September 1852 his wife Ann became the licence holder, giving the address as Top Bank. Ann did not stay long and Matthew Bell became the licence holder in 1854 the address was again No. 3 East Street. Matthew stayed for twenty years. On 31 December 1873, not long after Richard Gillard had taken over the inn, an explosion occurred when the clock attached to the fountain in front of the inn was about to be lit. The explosion of gas destroyed the clock and the roof of the fountain was badly damaged. Through the accident Richard Gillard's son had his face severely burned. In 1936 Tynemouth magistrates granted an application made on behalf of Mrs Carruthers, owner of the inn, to carry out alterations including a lounge, dining room, five bedrooms and conveniences. This resulted in Tynemouth Council giving outline planning for the widening of East Street on the west side. In 1959 Hammond United Breweries Ltd were the owners of the hotel, advertising 'Guards Ales' in all the bars, Export Unity, and 'Best Scotch Bitter' drawn from the wood. In May 1985 a new look was given to the 200-year-old inn, 'sizzling scarlet and seductive black' was how it was described at the time. Bass North spent £150,000 to provide a cocktail bar, which overlooked the long sands and the sea. It had been named the 'Breakers', a lounge with a light and sound system upstairs with a carvery restaurant downstairs. The revamp had altered the inside beyond recognition: the dining room had been resited and doors

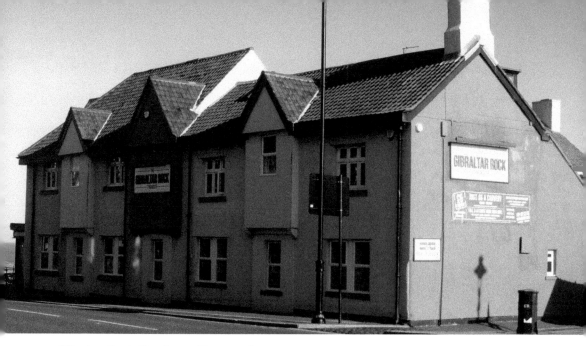

Gibraltar Rock, East Street, Tynemouth.

were removed, with even the tenants Ray and Jean Delaney confessing to getting lost at times. In October 1995 more than £500 worth of damage was caused when an arsonist set fire to both toilet rolls and holders in the gentlemen's toilets. In 1997 the Rock was the area finalist for the North East Bass Taverns National Catering Award. The Gibraltar Rock has an excellent view from the dining room of the coast and the priory.

58. Rose of Allendale

This quaint property was advertised by Robert Nicholson in 1846 as the Rose of Allendale Inn. On Monday 9 August 1847 the inn was put up for auction at the Half Moon Inn, Bigg Market whether it sold or not is unclear as Robert stayed at the inn until 1853 when Ellen Ferguson became the licensee. At an auction held at the Albion Hotel, North Shields on 14 October 1873, Lot 10 comprised of the Rose of Allendale, beer house, with house and warehouse behind, together with a shop being bought by a Mr Dewer for £560. In September 1879 the inn was once again being auctioned. It was described as containing 'an excellent bar and parlour on the ground; long room 25 feet long, with two recess closets on the first floor: and Four attics, two with dormer windows: Kitchen and large vaulted cellar in the basement the latter extending beyond the building under the yard, to a large extent with a hatch in the lane, at the side of the premises.' On 1 June 1923 the Justices of the borough of Tynemouth met as Compensation Authority to consider the question of renewing the licenses of five of the pubs in Tynemouth. The Rose of Allendale, the Prudhoe Hotel, the Seven Stars and the Union Tavern all in Percy Street, and the Priory Inn East Street. After just 16 minutes deliberation, the Mayor remarked that

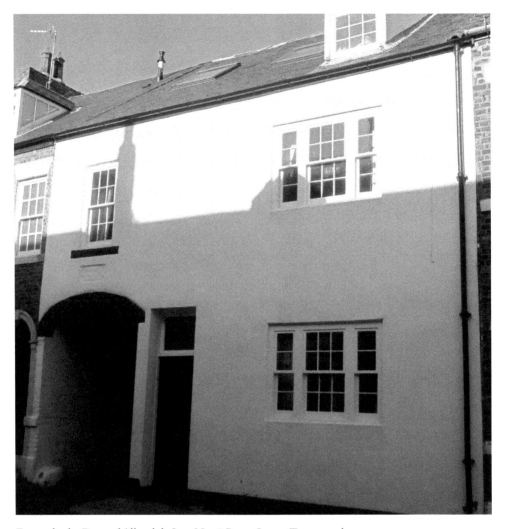

Formerly the Rose of Allendale Inn, No. 8 Percy Street, Tynemouth.

after careful consideration all licence renewals were refused. On 21 July 1924 the Rose of Allendale was closed down along with the other three public houses in Percy Street, the Seven Stars, the Prudhoe Hotel and the Union Tavern. The Priory Inn on East Street was also closed down on that day.

59. Grand Hotel

On 30 June 1877 the Grand Hotel was up for sale or let. It was advertised as being completed of elegant stone. Having been built for Major W. H. Allison Esq., JP, of Undercliffe at a cost of £20,000, its situation was unequalled by any other marine hotel in England. It was fully licenced and its interior furnished in an elaborate and luxurious manner. It comprised of: a basement, ground floor, first-, second-, third- and fourth-floors, with the usual sitting rooms, coffee room, conservatory and anteroom, ball room billiard room, forty bedrooms, two refreshment bars, complete kitchen, excellent stabling and good cellar accommodation. Its close proximity to the Winter Gardens, priory, skating rink, bathing beach, aquarium and pier made it quite popular with the Victorians. The *Shields Daily News*, on 8 June 1878, advertised the Grand Hotel as being the largest in the north-east of England and said it was to be opened to the public on Monday 1 July, although the public bar and a refreshment room had been open for several days. There were first- and second-class dining rooms. The staircase leading from the first-floor entrance to each floor was an important feature of the interior, dividing the hotel into two parts. Nicholas Daniels became the licensee and in June 1879. Mr Bourgogne, an experienced chef, became the manager. Monday 2 June 1884 saw the annual meeting of the North Eastern Bicycle Meet take place at Tynemouth, and after the club they assembled at Percy Park and the procession proceeded to Cullercoats and back. After a photograph was taken they adjourned to the hotel for dinner. On Wednesday 19 November 1890 Tynemouth Priory Cycling Club held their annual dinner in the hotel, which was attended by over a hundred members and guests. On Friday 23 January 1891 the first 'Cinderella Dance' was held at the hotel. This was to become a fortnightly event, promoted by the Mayor Alderman Whitehorn and other prominent gentlemen. On 23 July 1931 the hotel

Grand Hotel, Grand Parade, Tynemouth.

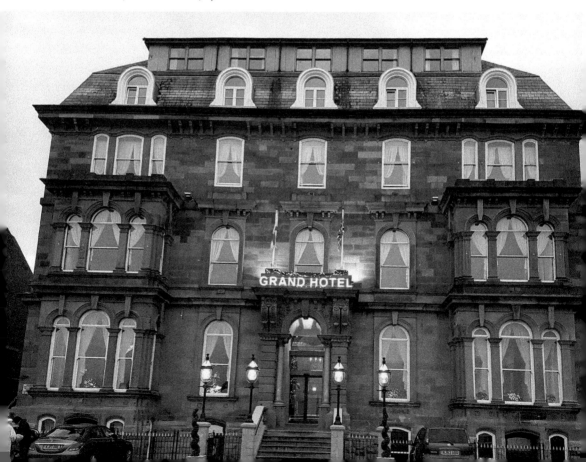

was sold by public auction to Mr J. G. Radcliffe for £10,000. The bid was accepted, although it was the only one made. In February 1952 at a Valentine party at the hotel the Mayoress Councillor Mrs T. A. M. Hails played a slave girl and deputy mayor, Councillor A. R. Vella, as Leprosy, Cleopatra's mother, in a re-enactment of *Anthony and Cleopatra*. The funds were in aid of the Mayoress Charities Appeal. Today the hotel has a warm, friendly atmosphere and staff are very friendly, although it has been altered over the years it still retains its air of 'olde world' splendour. The lower floor is called the Chambers and is where events are held. The dance floor holds 200. The first floor caters for weddings and its dance floor holds 150. Only the top floors are used as guest bedrooms.

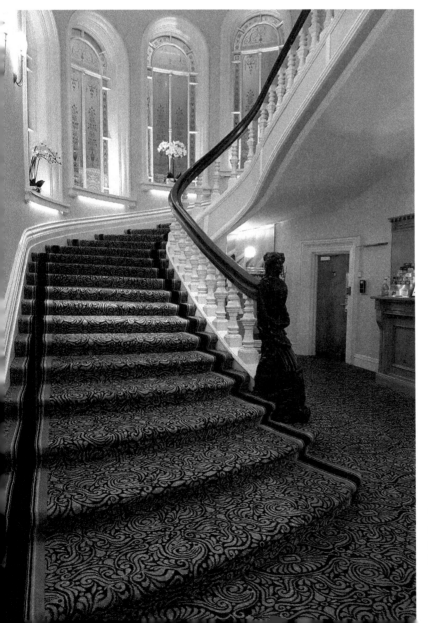

The grand staircase with a beautiful lady carved at the end of the banister.

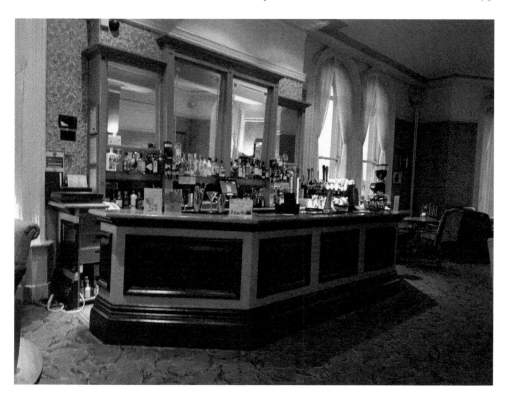

Above: The sitting room with its central bar for clientele, a selection of sofas, armchairs and a coffee table to the left, with tables and chairs to the right.

Right: One of the dining rooms on the ground floor.

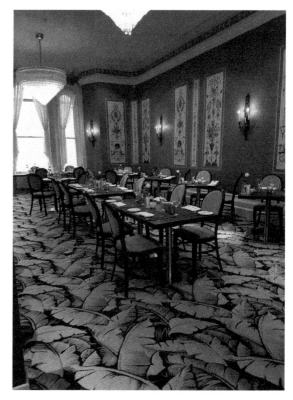

60. Copperfields

Copperfields Bar is part of the Grand Hotel and is accessible by a short passage to the left of the reception area in the hotel or by an entrance on Hotspur Street. Over the years it has been known by several different names, such as Clachan Bar and Troll Bar. Now selling real ales from both local and national breweries, it is quite popular. It is set on two levels – the upper with comfortable seating, the lower being the bar area. This spacious but comfortable bar has a warm friendly atmosphere and friendly staff. Copperfields is ideal for popping into after a walk along Tynemouth Beach as all are welcome, including your dog.

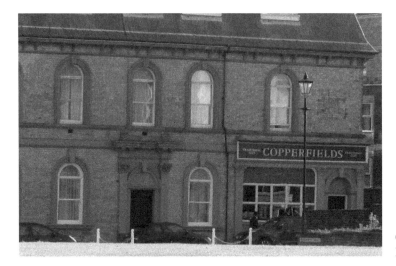

Copperfields, Hotspur Terrace.

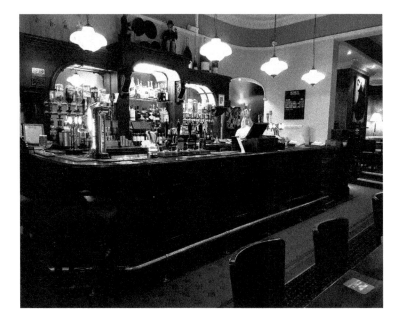

Copperfields' elegant bar.

61. Park Hotel

In a picturesque spot overlooking the sea the Park Hotel was opened on 1 July 1939. The hotel comprised of a luxurious and beautifully decorated lounge and restaurant on the ground floor with the hotel lounge and ballroom. A bar, buffet and sitting rooms were located on the south-facing frontage. On the first floor were thirty residential bedrooms, and two lavender suites were fitted with hot and cold water and central heating. A dining room for residents, two large sitting rooms and a lounge lead off the hall on this floor for the comfort of the guests. The hotel was bound on three sides by a large outside terrace, and a bowling green was to be laid out on the west side along with garages. In 1982 the hotel was sold to five local businessmen: Terry Dene, Peter McDonald, James Turnbull, Ronald Arris and Richard Pickering. On 6 December 1994 a 'Stars in Your Eyes' event was staged at the hotel. Tyneside Charitable Trust for Heart Disease and Diabetes staged the event, which saw Shirley Bassey impersonator Maxine Barrie and Dieter Graham as Elton John perform. Tickets were £9.50, which included a meal and the money raised went to making Christmas happy for the children's wards of the local hospitals. A concert in aid of the Support Centre for Deaf Children based at Monkhouse Primary School was performed by the Ravenswood Singers and organised by the Rotary Club of Tynemouth. In August 2000 Sewa Singh Gill, a regular drinker in the hotel, after seeing it deteriorate over the years, bought the hotel when it was advertised for sale, carrying out substantial work on it. In 2018 the hotel underwent a £3 million refurbishment. It now boasts spacious executive suites with a guest room, deluxe bedrooms, standard bedrooms, family rooms, a breakfast room, a light and airy hotel bar, meeting facility, banquet hall, outdoor banquet area and smoking area.

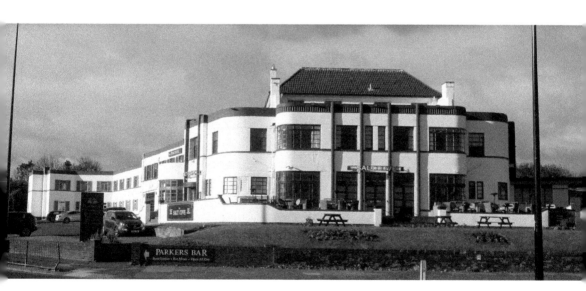

Park Hotel, Grand Parade, Tynemouth.

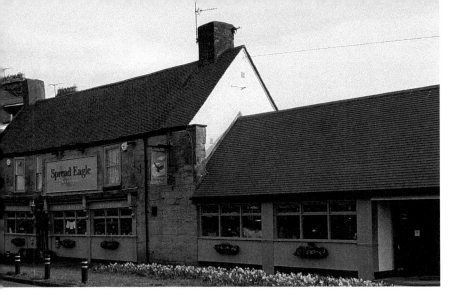

The Spread Eagle Inn, Front Street, Preston Village.

62. Spread Eagle

Matthew Arthur advertised the Spread Eagle Inn in 1822. On Tuesday 19 February 1861 at the George Tavern in King Street, North Shields, the inn was for sale by auction, together with the large garden attached, containing 3,360 square yards. It was in the occupation of Messrs T. D. Davison & Company. In September 1883 the inn was to let with immediate possession. On 28 June 2003 the inn reopened after a three and a half week closure for extensive refurbishment. The bar was extended to give landlady Margaret Appleby more space where home-made food was to be served. In November 2017 licensee Claire Hall won the Best Food Pub in the national awards run by Heineken, owned Star Pubs and Bars. This was their second win. A Cask Marque accreditation for the quality of their beer was given only the week before.

63. The Sportsman

The Sportsman's Arms has been associated with the village of Preston for more than 200 years and is thought to have derived its name from the annual road race that was held as part of the Preston Hopping. This event lasted from Saturday to Monday and would not only include parades but all manner of races – pony, donkey, later bicycle and, of course, the famous road race, which would finish at the inn. The original pub stood in North Road only yards from where the present one now stands. Ephraim Nicholson advertised the inn in 1844, but on 19 February 1864 Ephraim was found hanged in the stable connected to the house; he was over seventy years of age. On 1 July 1876 Joseph Blacklock, publican at the inn, was summoned before the licensing committee for allowing drunkenness on 17 June. The man in question was Owen Maran, a painter who after working very hard all week and found himself unable to get into his lodgings had fallen asleep, but was not drunk. The case was dismissed. In June 2010, despite objections from nearby residents, landlord Peter Johnson, chairman of the Pubwatch Scheme, was granted an extension to the Sportsman's licence, which included live music and dancing. The pub opens until 3 a.m. on New Year's Eve. Meals at the Sportsman are home-cooked, which I found out to my delight when I popped in one day. The staff were really friendly and helpful.

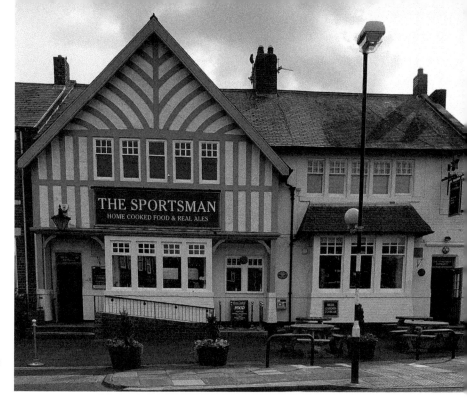

Sportsman,
Front Street,
Preston
Village.

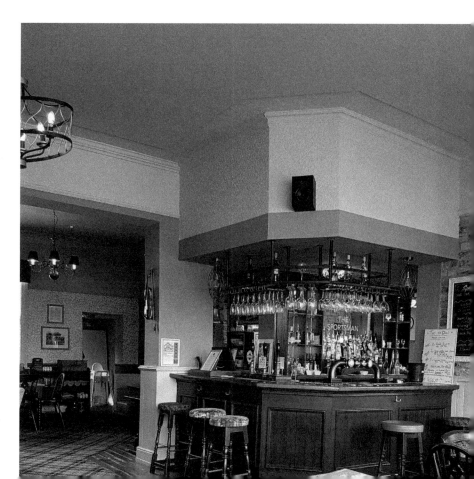

The
Sportsman.

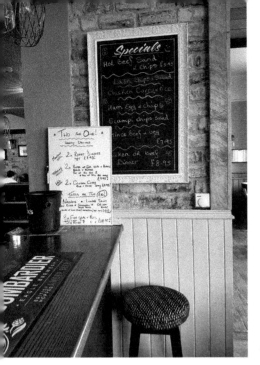

The Sportsman's specials board.

64. Fox Hunter

Thomas Craig, a sergeant in the Northumberland Yeomanry Cavalry, advertised the Fox Hunter Inn in 1834. Thomas had apparently changed the name of the pub, which, according to W. Harold Smurthwaite, had originally been called the Plane Tree in honour of the hunt, where hares were the quarry of choice at the time until at Christmastide when fox hunting took over. On Monday 15 January 1849 the inn was auctioned at John Scott's, Duke of Granby Inn, North Shields. Sales details reveal the freehold inn consisted of four rooms, a bar, cellar, office and a four-roomed cottage adjoining – both in the occupation of Thomas Craig as tenant. In 1850 John Richardson was the licensee. In 1880 the inn was to let, 'rent and ingoings' moderate', and Carr and Brewers were the owners. In January 1883 the inn was again to let from the February term. In 1939 the original Fox Hunter closed and the licence was transferred to this present inn. In 1944 the licensee Cecil John Grinton was fined 40s at Tynemouth Police Court for showing lights from the inn, which was against the blackout regulations. In 1946 the Fox Hunter was a Newcastle Breweries Blue Star inn. Water from an open-cast coal site is thought to have caused the flood in the cellar of the inn on 3 May 1952 when the fire brigade pumped out 6 inches using a wheelbarrow pump. Luckily the liquor supplies were unharmed. In January 1983 manager Mike Barlow was now not only giving his clientele beer on draught but also milk, which was not only sold straight but could be made into milk cocktails or used as a mixer. Mike had found out about the milk from his local Dairy Crest supplier at Whitley Bay. In May 1993 the Fox Hunter underwent major refurbishment with Scottish and Newcastle and opened as one of their new style 'Homespeads' restaurants. In November 1993 the law changed and for the first time children under the age of fourteen were allow into pubs – the Fox Hunter was one of the first to do

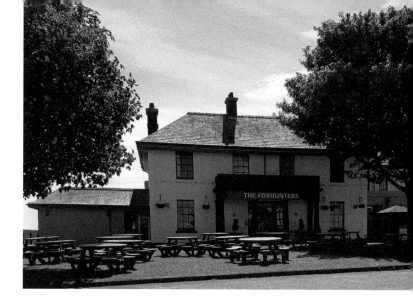

The Fox Hunter,
Preston Gate.

so. The Fox Hunter, being both stylish and spacious, included a soft play room that was well equipped, having a ball pool and a colourful outdoor playground. There is a child's toilet and excellent facilities for nappy changing, and a children's special menu. On 12 June 1997 Ian Carey applied to the Petty Sessional Division of North Tyneside for a New Justices' Licence, which would give him the authority to sell intoxicating liquor of all descriptions for consumption both on and off the premises. In 2018 the Fox Hunter again underwent a six-figure refurbishment, with a new back bar and separate areas for dining and watching the latest sport on television. The colour scheme has introduced a combination of natural wood, colour and textures, creating a modern finish. Its contemporary flooring, new tiles and stylish fittings create a brighter environment for clientele, all of which made for a successful reopening for this very popular public house.

65. The Wheat Sheaf

When first built the Wheat Sheaf Inn on Rakes Lane, New York, was mostly surrounded by farmland. Today not much has changed as it remains surrounded by fields and still sits on the old main road. On 27 August 1827 an auction for Wheat and Oats was held at the house of Alex Barrass. 'Alexander Barras' advertised the inn in 1828 and the address was simply 'New York'. In February 1849 the inn was for sale. The inn and close were in the hands of landlord Mr Towns at an annual rent of £46. Cuthbert Stobbs, who was also a carter, was the landlord in 1854. In 1873 Cuthbert gave the address as Murton. Cuthbert stayed at the inn until Walter Logan became the licensee in 1886, giving the address as New York, Chirton. Walter died at the inn in December 1907. On 20 September 1938 the licence for the inn, which was formerly held by her husband, the late Robert Taylor, was granted to Mrs Mary D. Taylor along with the music and singing licence. In 1996 after being extensively refurbished it still retained that cosy atmosphere with a reasonably priced menu and a wide range of Scottish and Newcastle beers. Today it still had a number of beers but also caters for the family with meals to suit every taste.

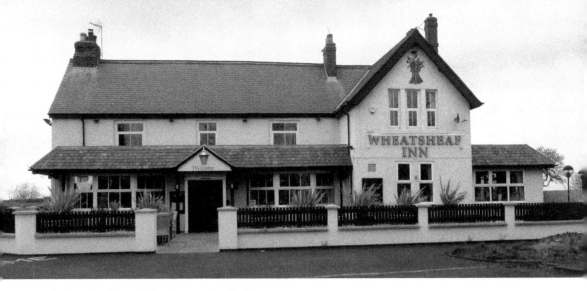

Wheatsheaf Inn, Rakes Lane, New York.

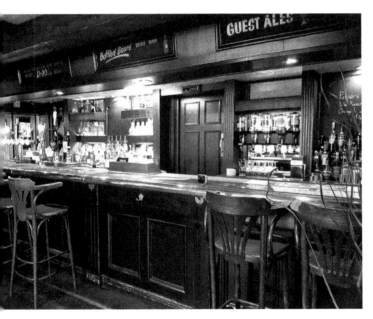

Central bar.

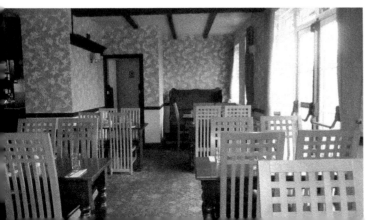

Raised dining area.

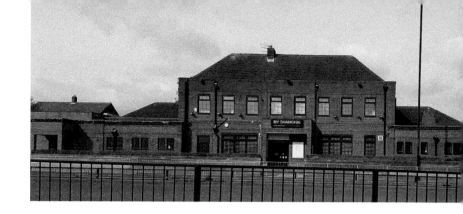

My Shanghi, formerly the Cannon Inn, Billy Mill.

66. Cannon Inn

The original Cannon Inn was at Chirton Hill, not far from where this now stands. John Dobson, farmer and cartwright advertised the Cannon in 1853. As John was a farmer it is most likely the original inn was a converted farm building. When James King advertised the Cannon in 1871 he gave the address as Billy Mill, Chirton. In September 1927 North Shields purchased Chirton Hill Farm, which included the Cannon Inn and went ahead to make the necessary application to have the inn registered in their name. The new Cannon was built on the Tynemouth Coast Road, which itself was also new at the time.

Opened on 30 July 1935, this new type of public house was the first approaching the idea of a road house in the Tynemouth area. This Georgian-style building was designed by Messrs T. A. Page, Son & Bradbury and built by North Shields builder Benjamin Peel. It offered enjoyment in pleasant surroundings with a gravel space to one side for cars. Inside the floor was parquet covered and the walls had light oak panelling. The latest type of beer engine was on the counter with ebony-handled levers that drew the beer up from the cellar through telescopic pipes. In 1985 the inn became Whitbread Hambleton Inn's biggest development in the north-east that year. Derek and Margaret Yellop became the licensees and the inn went from strength to strength. In 1992 extra car parking spaces were provided for clientele. On 2 April 1996 the inn hosted a coffee morning for the North East Promenarders Against Cancer with a raffle and tombola stall, which was a great success. Tickets were 50p with coffee and biscuits included. Unfortunately the Cannon became another public house that suffered a decline, with people spending more time drinking at home or in the nightclubs.

67. Pineapple Inn

This was originally the home of John and Margaret Dobson. John was an affluent market gardener at the time of his son's birth. It was not until 1828 that Margaret Dobson advertised the Pineapple as an inn, although it had been known as Dobson's Inn when John Dobson Jr was growing up. On Wednesday 4 March 1874 a ball was held at the inn on the occasion of the Quadrille party held there for the winter. In 1875 Charles Edward Minns became the licensee. On the morning of 9 May 1888 Charles Edward Minns was found hanging by his neck in the pantry of their home – he was fifty-five years old. In March 1983 schoolgirls Angela Duffy and Michelle Whitley

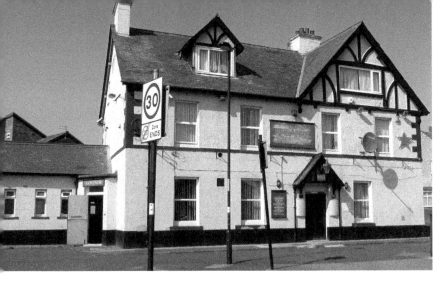

Pineapple Inn, Chirton, birthplace of the architect John Dobson.

tried to brighten up their area. Wanting to remove the graffiti from the pub proved a much bigger task than expected. Fred and Bedellia Smith were waiting for the brewery to redecorate and thought that although it did not make much difference they got top marks for effort. In November 1996 the inn was so neglected that it was boarded up and the owners were reprimanded for neglecting it. On 8 May 1998 Jacqueline Foster applied to the Licensing Sessions at North Tyneside Court for the licence to run the Pineapple, which she had been running for the previous six months.

68. The Ridges

In 1938 plans for a proposed hotel on Waterville Road and Minton Lane by J. H. Morton and Son for R. H. Morton were approved under the byelaws, of the Town and Country Planning Order 1933, but were adjourned. On 18 May 1938 the Finance Committee heard the report on the proceedings of the Augmented Sub-Committee held on 13 May into the suggested transfer from the Corporation of the Licence of the Wheatsheaf public house which they owned, to a site on the Ridges Estate. After a long drawn out affair and getting a dispensation from the Duke of Northumberland for a spirit licence, on 25 January 1939 T. A. Page, Son and Bradbury applied for a licence for the proposed premises now West Percy Road and Waterville Road, Ridges estate. The Ridges Inn opened on Tuesday 16 April 1940, built for William McEwan and Co. Ltd, Fountain Brewery, Edinburgh and City Road, Newcastle. The new inn had three public rooms, a bar, sitting room and buffet as well as out-sales. A very large cellar for storing the beer and up-to-date lavatories. In December 1969, in a bid to improve the inn, which had got a bit of a stigma, Scottish and Newcastle Breweries who now owned it decided on a change of name. Councillor Charles Carter, leader of the fight to improve the image thought The Meadow Inn a good name, but the breweries thought 'The Robins' in honour of North Shields football team. Customers at the Robin, Chirton, thought this would lead to confusion, so the breweries decided on the Sein Boat, which was a type of fishing boat, many of which operated from North Shields at the time.

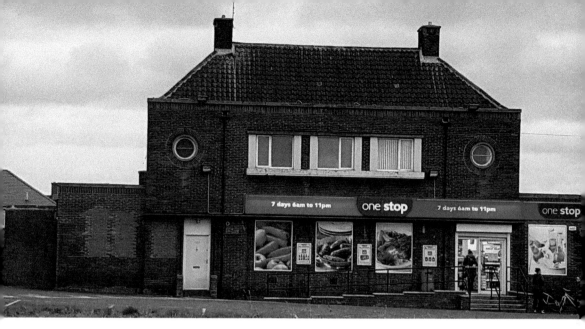

Formerly the Ridges Inn, Waterville Road and Minton Lane.

69. The Redburn

The Redburn situated beside the roundabout on Waterville Road and Wallsend Road received the transferred licence of the Marquis of Granby, Church Street, North Shields on 17 December 1956 after an inspection of the premises. The application was made by Mr C. P. Rea on behalf of William Younger & Co. Ltd. The stone building was once the vicarage of St John's Church, which dates back to the 1870s. Closed in 1995 by Newcastle Breweries, it was reopened again in 2001 when bought by the present owner Sharon. Having undergone extensive refurbishment it is now a friendly pub for the family to enjoy a night out. It is open from 11.00–00.00. Food is also served.

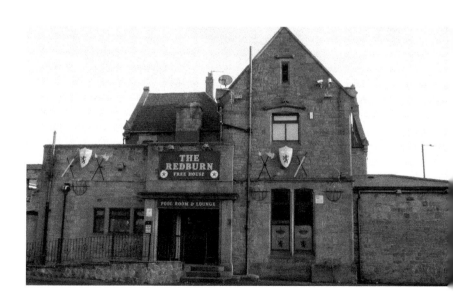

The Redburn,
Percy Main.

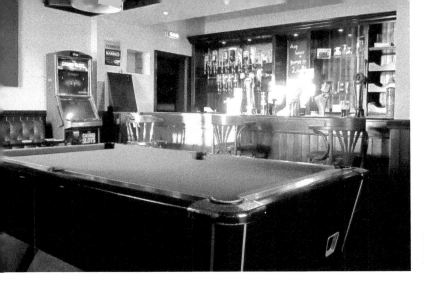

Small bar to the left of the door on Waterville Road.

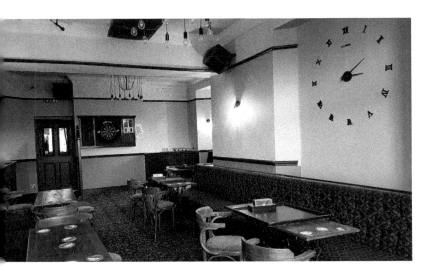

Lounge with dartboard to the right.

70. Percy Arms

It is not until 1853 that Thomas Bowman advertised the Percy Arms Inn as Percy Main. His wife Jane became the licensee in 1873 after his death. In August 1990 Scottish and Newcastle sold the Percy Arms to Go-Ahead Northern Bus Company; little changed for the tenants except the ordering process, which Jean and Bob Hindson then had to phone over to Go-Ahead Northern who in turn passed it on the S & N. On Saturday 26 February 1994 a charity night in aid of leukaemia research was organised by Pauline Wallis whose son Sam had been getting treatment for over two years. In November 1994 David Ross & Co. had the Percy Arms up for sale, being described as a 'detached stone built property with public bar, lounge and function room. 3 bed flat. Car parking is to front. Former tenanted house for sale, thought to trade about £2,000 a week, Freehold sale. Offers around £85,000'. In February 2010 it was known as PJ's Hotel and when Paul and Jennifer Jarvis sold the hotel they offered a donation of £100,000 to St Oswald's Hospice. It then became known as 'Sambuca'.

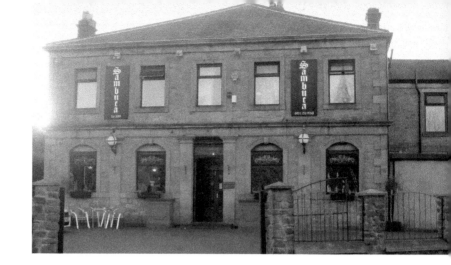

Sambuca restaurant – originally the Percy Arms/ Percy Main.

71. Wolsington House

A sad reflection of the times; the Wolsington House Hotel now stands almost alone. In 1834 John Veitch advertised the hotel with the lovely address of Mount Pleasant. On Friday 30 September 1887 an inquest was held into the death of Archibald McPhail, who had drowned in a water tank in the backyard of his parent's house in Lawson Street on the Wednesday afternoon. Archibald had slipped into the yard while a servant, who had been washing clothes in the yard had been called into the kitchen, he unfortunately fallen into the well. Verdict was 'Accidental drowning'. In 1901 the Wolsington House was rebuilt and during that time the National Independent Order of Oddfellows, Loyal Earle Percy Lodge who normally held there meeting at the hotel arranged to hold their meetings at the Sir Colin Campbell Hotel every alternate Monday when contributions would be collected. In 1991 the reformed Jazz Bands Vieux Carre who were better known for playing at the New Orleans Jazz Club in the 1950s and early 1960s. Ian Heslop, Peter Coles, Chas Coles, Peter Gascoigne, Davy Rae and Ronny Robinson were playing at the Wolsington every Thursday night. In 1992 the hotel was bought by Go Ahead Leisure. In May 1995 the tenancy was on

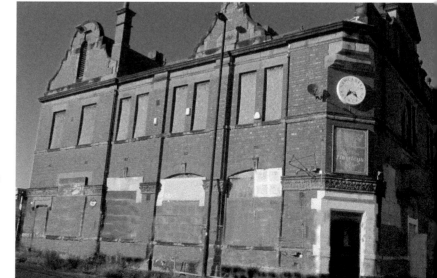

A sad-looking Wolsington House Hotel, Appleby Street and Burdon Main Road.

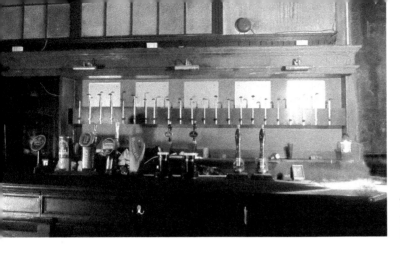

The bar inside the hotel, which would have been fully stocked at one time.

offer with the ingoing being £8,000. Standing almost at the entrance of Smiths Docks it was one of the first to suffer from the closure, closing in 2011.

72. Berwick Arms

In Christie's 1871 directory, David Cockburn is listed as a beer retailer, Trinity Street, it is not until Ward's 1875–76 that David advertised the Berwick Arms Inn at No. 19 Trinity Terrace. Joseph Emerson became the licensee in 1879. On Sunday 7 May 1989 manager Dave Patton surprised his regulars, for instead of the usual cheese and biscuits on offer at the bar, offers of what was virtually a five-course meal was made. Tandoori chicken, barbeque spare ribs, roast potatoes, black pudding, crisps as well as the usual cheese, biscuits and nuts were to prove very popular. Dave, his wife Susan, who prepared the food, saw their sales increased by almost 50 percent. The inn with its lovely terracotta faience tile work was for a brief time called the Trinity's. In May 2010 Peter Borrow applies for a licence for films, live music, late night refreshments, and alcohol, for 10.30 to 24.00 hours Monday to Saturday and Sundays 11.00 to 23.30 hours;

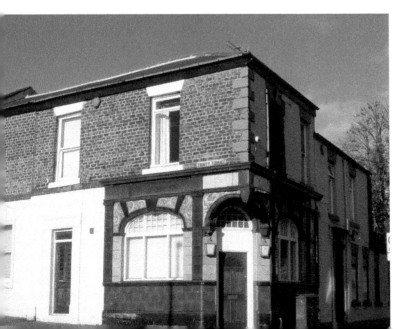

Formerly the Berwick Arms, Trinity Street.

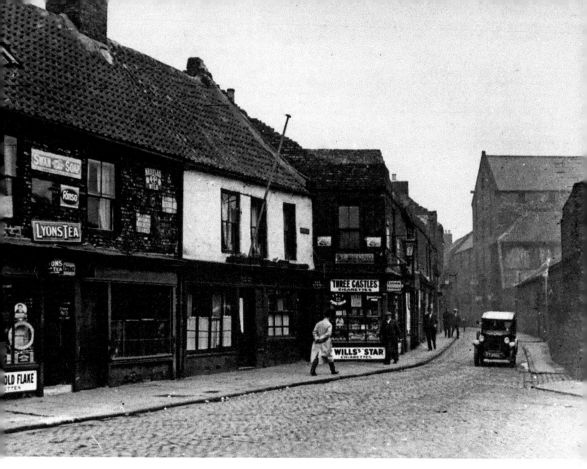

Duke Street, looking east from the Bull Ring.

with seasonal variations. Peter was the last landlord before it became a casualty of the decline in the shipping industry.

73. Turk's Head and 74. Phoenix

By the time this photograph was taken in the 1930s Duke Street had only a few public houses left. In 1934 the only public houses left were the Crane House Vaults, Phoenix both Newcastle Breweries. In 1890 there was Essex Arms (Robert Turnbull), No. 23 at the beginning of Duke Street from the Bull Ring, with the Turk's Head (Thomas Hedley), No. 33, the Phoenix Inn (Mrs Sarah Miller), No. 41, Crane House, Thomas Walker, No. 50 and the Ferry House, belonging to James Miller – No. 1 on the left. When Magdalen Weatherstone first advertised the Turk's Head Tavern in 1822, Duke Street had many more taverns, Brandon Mill, Martin Wylam, Crown and Thistle, Thomas Herron, Hope and Anchor, Thomas Skelton, King's Arms, Jane Weatherburn, Steam Pocket, Richard Martin, Three Mariners, Turk's Head and the Yarmouth Arms. Many changed names over the years but all finally succumbed to changing times and many were demolished to make way for the expansion of the shipping industry after the First World War, unfortunately it was also the downfall of many others when shipping declined on the river.

75. Crane House

Mary Patten advertised the Phoenix in 1846 and in 1850 Isabella Blacklock gave the address as No. 32. Isabella kept the inn until 1861 when Duncan McLennon became the licensee, giving the address as No. 41. Duncan did not stay long as in 1865 Richard Weatherstone Gibb was the landlord, but in 1875 Mrs Mary Louisa Gibb was the licensee. Mary died on 9 February 1883, age sixty-five, and Richard and Mary's daughter took over the Phoenix keeping the licence until 1891.

Crane House, the only surviving public house in Duke Street although it has now been converted into flat. Advertised by Charles Dunn in 1834 the Crane House was put up for auction by Lamb and Edge on the 16 December 1838, described as 'a modern fully licensed hotel and dwelling house, situated opposite the Ferry'. By 1846 David Cooper was the licensee, David died in 1850 his wife Hannah became the licensee. Hannah married Thomas Stewart, a steamboat owner, on 22 January 1852; Thomas then took over the licence. In July 1856 Thomas advertised three-fourths of the Paddle Steamer Princess for sale by private treaty. On 12 July 1857 Hannah's daughter Barbra married Thomas Walker in South Shields and a few months later Thomas Stewart died. On 8 September 1858 Hannah Stewart advertised for sale the good Steamboat

Duke Street, looking west from New Quay. The Crane Hotel is on the right, with the Phoenix Inn a few doors away, and on the left is the Ferry House.

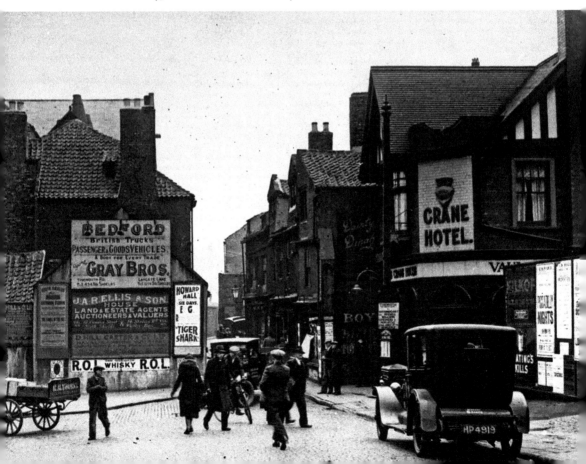

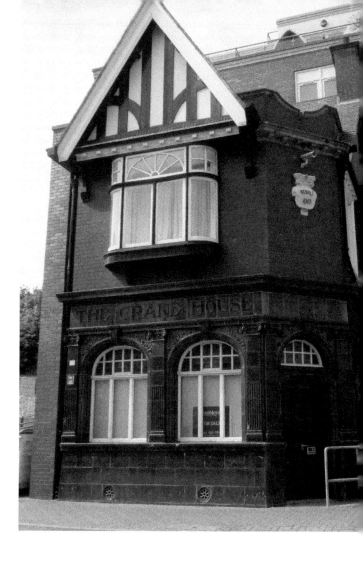

Crane House, Duke Street.

Princess, this was possibly the one share left that had belonged to her late husband. Thomas Walker took over the licence from Hannah. Barbra Walker died 18 January 1891 in the pub age fifty-six years. Thomas stayed until William McConnell became the licence holder in 1896. An application for the transfer of the music licence to Catherine Robinson from that of her late husband on 18 April 1950 was granted. After a slump in business through repair works Alan Kelly, manager successfully claimed £6,000 compensation from Northumberland Water. In June 2005 construction workers moved in to convert the old Crain House into fifteen luxury apartments.

76. Ferry Mews

According to the 1865 Ordinance Survey map of North Shields the Ferry House Inn was a small building at the back of what became the Tyne Harbour Masters headquarters until 1972. Richard Martin advertised the Steam Pocket in Duke Street in 1822; in 1834 Richard Wylam had changed the name to the Steam Ferry House. When Margaret Wilson took over in 1844 she gave the address as New Quay. George

Hunter gave the address in 1846 as the Market Place. Landlords did not stay long: in 1851 the inn had another landlord, John Atkinson. On Friday 2 July 1852 the Steam Ferry Co. held their annual general meeting at the inn. A 10 per cent dividend was declared on the original capital. On Sunday 16 August 1857 John Atkinson suddenly died and his wife Jane became the licensee and in 1861 became known as the Ferry House. Jane stayed until 1867 making her the longest licensee. Enoch R. D. Halder became the landlord, staying only until 1872 when James Miller became the landlord. James died on 15 May 1888 at only forty-five years. On 10 April 1891 a meeting of the River Tyne Commission was held and agreed to let the Ferry House Inn from the 1 August to Mr Borthwick of Newcastle for £250 per annum. In August 1892 the River Tyne Commission agreed to repairs and considered pulling down the inn and rebuilding, the matter was left in the hands of the Harbour and Ferry Committee. In 1896 W. Marshall & Sons became the new licensees of the inn it was not advertised again and later became utilised as offices in connection with the Ferry.

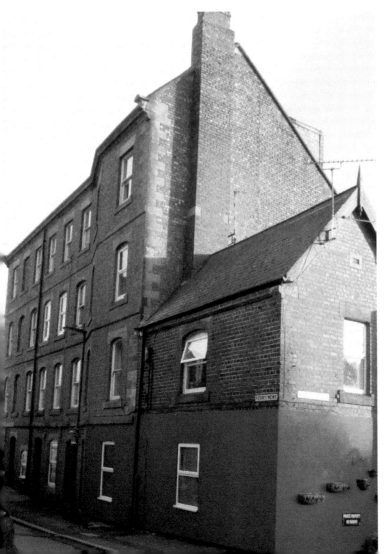

Possibly the old Ferry House Inn, New Quay.